DESIGNING A SCHOOL LIBRARY MEDIA CENTER FOR THE FUTURE

SECOND EDITION

Rolf Erikson and Carolyn Markuson

American Library Association
Chicago   2007

While extensive effort has gone into ensuring the reliability of information appearing in this book, the publisher makes no warranty, express or implied, on the accuracy or reliability of the information, and does not assume and hereby disclaims any liability to any person for any loss or damage caused by errors or omissions in this publication.

Cover photo of the Bruce and Patrice Buxton Library at Falmouth Academy courtesy of Susan D. Moffat.

Composition in Janson and Tekton MM by ALA Editions using InDesign CS on a PC platform.

The paper used in this publication meets the minimum requirements of American National Standard for Information Sciences—Permanence of Paper for Printed Library Materials, ANSI Z39.48-1992. ∞

Library of Congress Cataloging-in-Publication Data
Erikson, Rolf.
    Designing a school library media center for the future / Rolf Erikson
and Carolyn Markuson. — 2nd ed.
        p.   cm.
    Includes bibliographical references and index.
    ISBN-13: 978-0-8389-0945-4 (alk. paper)
    ISBN-10: 0-8389-0945-0 (alk. paper)
    1. Instructional materials centers—United States—Design and construction.
    2. Instructional materials centers—United States—Automation. 3. School libraries—
United States—Design and construction. 4. School libraries—United States—Automation.
    I. Markuson, Carolyn Bussian. II. Title.
        Z675.S3E75 2007
        027.80973—dc22   2006037644

ISBN-10: 0-8389-0945-0
ISBN-13: 978-0-8389-0945-4

Printed in the United States of America

11   10   09   08   07   5   4   3   2   1

CONTENTS

FIGURES

FOREWORD

Considerable research evidence shows that school libraries are vital to students' education. This research, which spans almost four decades, demonstrates that many factors contribute to the establishment and operation of effective school libraries that support student learning and achievement. These factors include adequate and appropriate information resources, state-of-the-art information technology infrastructure, and, most importantly, essential pedagogical leadership in enabling students to learn in complex information environments.

The fusion of print and electronic information environments now places considerable responsibility on learners to navigate this complex and often ambiguous information space, to locate pertinent information, to make judgments about the quality of the information, to make sense of the multiple perspectives, and to construct their own understanding of their chosen topics. If school libraries are to be effective transformational spaces where students are empowered to synthesize myriad pieces of information into personal knowing, and not merely information depositories, then it is increasingly important that school leaders, including school librarians, grapple with how to design and provide learning environments in school libraries that best foster the development of deep knowledge and deep understanding and that enable students to succeed and achieve through their schooling.

Well-designed learning environments in education settings take into account many factors: they are learner-centered, safe, comfortable, accessible, flexible, and equitable. The challenge of designing the school library to meet these dimensions as well as to be a multidimensional, whole-school learning space able to meet diverse information needs, learning styles, learning tasks, and instructional approaches needs considerable and careful thought. The learner must be at the heart of a well-designed school library. Although information sources, information services, and information technology are essential components of the school library and need deliberate consideration in the design process, they are not the center of the library.

A well-designed library facility is important, for multiple reasons. A well-designed school library facilitates an effective library program. Conversely, a poorly designed facility can impede a program's effectiveness and success. A well-designed library provides both an aesthetically compelling and an intellectually engaging place for students that motivates them to be in the library, to learn through the library, and to maximize their opportunities for success. A well-designed library creates a personalized learning space for students, a safe place for information encounters and for intervention and feedback in the information-to-knowledge process, and one that fosters pride and ownership in their school. A well-designed school library weaves the virtual and physical learning spaces, the human and technical interventions into an informational, transformational, and formational home base for every learner. Designing such a home base cannot be left to chance, intuition, or limited knowledge.

Design must be a collaborative process, drawing on multiple expertises and experiences. School librarians clearly do bring expertise to this process: they know how students learn through information, individually, in groups, and in classes, and how this learning is best maximized through the infrastructure, organization, management, and spatial arrangement of information resources. They know technology as well as work flows and learning flows. Yet high-performance design involves much more than this. It involves building ecology, site, energy, acoustic, and aesthetic considerations, to name a few. Specialized professional expertise may be needed to fill some gaps in knowledge of the process and its implementation. School librarians should not think they can or must do this on their own. Few, if any, school librarians are trained in facility design. Few school librarians have had one, let alone more than one, professional experience being involved in a school library design process. And often there is very little help from professional associations or schools of education. A new school library will be around for the next thirty years. We can't afford to make mistakes.

A fundamental principle of entering a school library design process is to recognize that it is very complex. The answer to a simple query on a school librarian electronic discussion list about some aspect of school library design is merely the beginning of a sustained dialogue, data-collection, and decision-making process, drawing on multiple sources of authority and expertise. The process also requires some well-honed negotiation skills. Too many school libraries are being designed solely by architects and school administrators. Often, their ideas are based on long-outdated premises about learning in rich and complex information environments. As a result, brand-new school libraries often look little changed from the school libraries of forty years ago. These costly and detrimental mistakes can be avoided by proactive and informed engagement in the design process. Such engagement calls for considerable assertiveness, sensitivity, and mutuality, with participants working together for common goals. It is a huge job, and it can be somewhat overwhelming in the context of the school librarian's already crowded days.

Designing a School Library Media Center for the Future provides a clear framework for all stakeholders to engage in the school library design process. In removing the mystique of school library design, it presents both the complexity and the collaborative nature of the design process as well as a pathway for meaningful engagement in this challenging responsibility. It is an exciting and worthwhile journey! And you begin the journey by walking it.

Dr. Ross J. Todd
Director of Research
Center for International Scholarship in School Libraries (CISSL)
School of Communication, Information and Library Studies
Rutgers, The State University of New Jersey

PREFACE

According to Rebuild America's Schools, at least one-third of K–12 schools in the United States need to be replaced or extensively repaired (see "Schools in Need," http://www.modernschools.org/need/). New schools are also needed to accommodate rising enrollments and to alleviate overcrowding. And so, over the next several years, many school librarians will find themselves involved with designing a new or renovated school library. If you work in a school that plans to build or renovate the library media facility, you, the school librarian, will be faced with both an enormous challenge and a tremendous opportunity. This is not to be taken lightly; it will be an opportunity to provide a library space for your students and staff that will enable the school's library program to be effectively carried out in an environment that is inviting, attracts users, and enhances the learning process. Moreover, because school buildings are meant to last a long time, the decisions you make will affect your library users for many years to come.

Today's school library has many functions and its design is complex, and the successful design of a school library requires a great deal of the school librarian. Although information relative to the topic can be gleaned from many sources, as all good librarians know, much of that information is useless or inaccurate. You may even get bad information from conference presentations. Before accepting the advice of another, look into that person's experience. Working on one (or even more than one) library facility project does provide valuable experience, but it is limited experience. Having worked on over eighty school library facility design projects since the mid-1980s, I have learned a great deal. And although I used to think I would eventually have all the answers, it just doesn't work that way; it is a continual learning process.

My first experience with designing a school library led me to believe that a well-designed, attractive, and inviting school library facility would have a positive effect on usage and student behavior and would enhance the learning that takes place within the library walls. Very little research has been done in this area, but what research exists confirms what I believed then and continue to believe. Combined with talented staff and exemplary programs, facilities can and do make a difference; even with talented staff and exemplary programs, poor facilities can detract from a program's effectiveness.

Yet, too many school library facilities continue to be poorly designed. Too many are riddled with serious mistakes. Too many fail to provide what students want because we have not included them in the planning process; as a result, we risk alienating our primary customer base. Too many fail to reflect what is known about learning and are designed in fundamentally the same way that school libraries were designed in the 1960s. We've made great strides in changing the role of the school librarian and in developing twenty-first-century programs, but changes in facilities have not kept pace. As a profession, we have spent more time and energy debating what to call ourselves and our school libraries than we have spent debating what our facilities need to be! If these mistakes in school library facility design continue, school libraries will become ineffective and irrelevant, and their very existence will be at risk.

My coauthor, Carolyn Markuson, and I hope that through this book, others who need to plan a new school library can benefit from what we have learned over the years. The book is written primarily for the librarian working at any level in the K–12 school environment; we also hope that school administrators, members of school library planning committees, architects, and those involved with the design of teen spaces for public libraries will find the book useful.

Because designing a new library facility most likely will be a once-in-a-lifetime experience, you may feel you have neither the time nor the inclination to pursue specialized training in library facility design. Although you may lack specific technical skills, in one area you are the expert: you know school libraries—how they function, the kinds of activities that take place in them, the types and quantities of materials and equipment they must house, the spaces they must provide, and how these spaces must relate to one another. This knowledge is critical to planning a successful new school library facility. Examples abound of school libraries where the planning and design were left to the "experts"—the architects, the interior designers, the building contractors—but where there was little or no involvement by the school librarian. It is in these examples where failures and sometimes outright disasters can be found.

You may be tempted to defer to those who seem better qualified. You may feel that you don't know anything about architecture or interior design, you can't read architectural blueprints, you've already too much to do—the list could go on and on. If you have any hope of ending up with a good school library, however, you must involve yourself at the very beginning, be involved at every stage of the process, and stay involved until the very end. You will need some skills this book cannot provide: you will need to be assertive in a way you may never have been before; you will need to bargain and negotiate skillfully; you will need extreme patience; you will need to find lots of time you most likely don't have; and, most of all, you will need a sense of humor.

Our goal is to demystify, to define, and to guide you through the process of school library design, from the realization that a new facility is likely to the point of completion. If you do the job well, rest assured you will feel a tremendous amount of pride and satisfaction.

Rolf Erikson

ACKNOWLEDGMENTS

The authors thank the following people who made significant contributions throughout the preparation of the second edition of *Designing a School Library Media Center for the Future:* Steven Arnoff, Susan Damerell, Lee Dore, and David Wood (Dore and Whittier Architects); Mary Ingham and Sarah Smith (Oak Point Associates); David Benn (Cho Benn Holback and Associates); Ross Todd; Patricia Velez; and Pjer Zanchi. Several individuals, companies, and organizations provided graphics and gave us permission to use copyrighted material without charge: we very much appreciate your assistance and generosity. We also wish to acknowledge our appreciation to our acquisitions editor Susan Veccia for her support and valuable advice. A special thank you goes to all of our many clients from the past several years. You have been our greatest teachers.

1

Seeing the Big Picture
What to Expect and When to Expect It

If you can dream it, you can do it.
—Walt Disney

Think big. A midwestern farm boy who began his career doodling and later went on to build the greatest entertainment network the world had ever known, Walt Disney is the epitome of imagination and determination. At the first hint of a possible new construction or renovation, you need to get involved and begin preparing. Unleash your imagination, roll up your sleeves, and get to work. If your facility is twenty or more years old, or if your school has become overcrowded, pay attention. Keep your ears open, because building plans can and do begin far in advance. Many schools conduct feasibility studies before a building program officially begins. These studies explore a number of variables and are designed to determine whether it is possible for a school to undertake a building project. Space and cost estimates are generated from a feasibility study, so your input is essential.

When you learn that you will be involved in the planning of a new library facility, your first question will likely be "Where do I begin?" You may feel totally overwhelmed. You could opt to scream and run, literally look for a different job. But it's unlikely any of us would pass up the opportunity to become involved with something so potentially rewarding. With an understanding of "the big picture," you can proceed logically, and you will know what to expect and when to expect it.

This chapter outlines the entire process, beginning at that moment when someone informs you that a new school library is in your future. The various steps, which can take two to four years, will be discussed in depth in later chapters. Figure 1-1 shows this process as a flowchart.

The Process

Educate Yourself (Self-Study)

If you are lucky, you will know that a new library project looms in the future. With this foresight, you can do some preliminary reading, talk with other school librarians who have experience with building projects, and visit some new school library facilities. If you have this head start, a chunk of your work is done and behind you. If not, the sooner you begin, the better. Obviously, you've already determined that a good place to begin is by reading this book. When

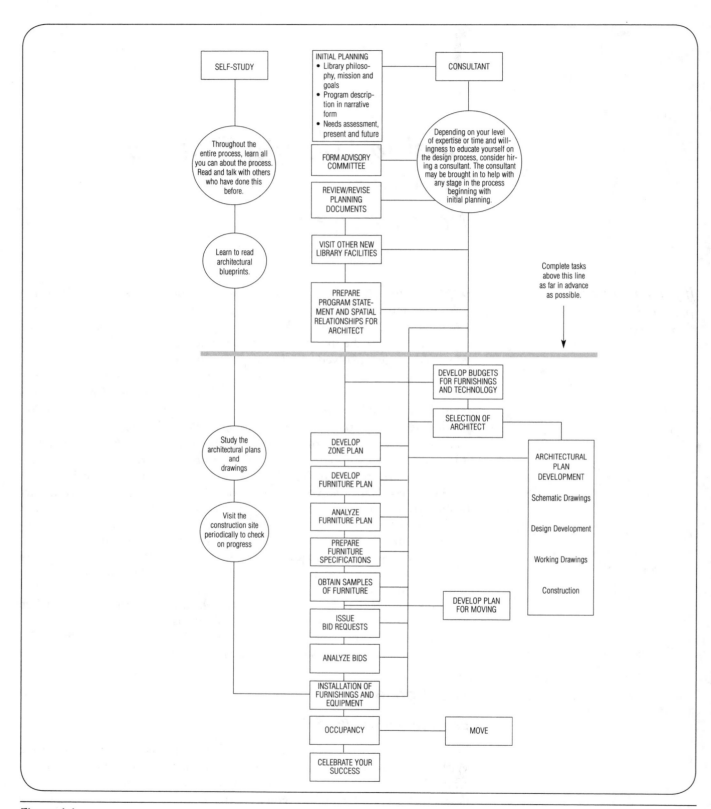

Figure 1-1

The Process of School Library Media Center Design

you put together a reading list, you may want to include the articles and publications in the Selected Readings section at the end of the book. If you are unfamiliar with architectural drawings, find a book that will help you understand the basics of reading blueprints. The more you read on the topic, the better equipped you'll be. Keep reading throughout the initial planning phase.

Hire a Consultant

If your school is willing to allocate funds, you would be well advised to hire or request that the architect hire a reputable consultant to help you through the process. State building assistance programs for school construction will often reimburse much of the cost of consultants as part of the architect's fees. Building a new library is expensive, and what is built must last and successfully serve its function for up to five decades or even more. A good consultant should be able to help you avoid costly errors, thereby justifying the additional expense. You should also check with your state education department. Many states offer resources to assist with school library building projects and may offer some consulting help. If you can't hire a professional consultant, at least try to obtain a second opinion on your furniture layout from a fellow school librarian.

Develop Program Documents (Initial Planning)

It is crucial that your library have in place the following program documents: a statement of philosophy, a mission statement, a goals outline, and a long-range strategic plan that includes a plan for technology. If you do not already have these documents, they must be completed now. No good facility planning can come out of a vacuum, and these documents will guide you and others responsible for the library design. See chapter 3 for more information.

Form an Advisory Committee

Establish a committee, separate from a building committee, to help with your role. If you already have a library advisory committee, you may elect to use it. This committee should represent your stakeholders: the faculty, staff, students, and parents. Consider including members of the community who are not parents; more and more, schools are planning new facilities that can

function as community centers. And keep in mind that all members of the community have a voice when matters of financing must be put to a vote.

Review and Revise Planning Documents

Chapter 3 describes the importance of program planning. If the library's planning documents were written before a new library facility was envisioned, these documents may need to be reviewed and revised. This is work you will want to do with your advisory committee.

Visit Other New Library Facilities

Take time to visit other schools that have recently built new facilities. Members of your advisory committee can help with this. Visit as many as you can; talk to the library staff, to students, and to teachers; take notes and pictures. Pay attention not only to what you like but also to what you dislike. You may want to visit some public libraries for ideas on furniture and layouts. Clip from magazines or find from Internet searches pictures of libraries that have features or a look you particularly like. It is well worth the effort to extend your visits beyond library facilities: visit bookstores, coffee shops, and other retail outlets where young people like to socialize and work.

Prepare a Program Statement for the Architect

Preparing a usable program statement is one of the most important tasks in the whole process. The program statement must translate your program documents (philosophy, mission, goals, and long-range plan) into layperson's terms and should be as concise as you can make it. The statement must include in narrative form a description of the library program, an assessment of both present and projected needs, inventories both of present materials and equipment and of proposed materials and equipment for expansion, and an estimate of the number of seats needed to accommodate students. Once the statement is written, have someone who is not a librarian and who is completely uninvolved with this project read the document. Then ask the person to tell you, in his or her own words, what it means. If it is confusing, go back to the drawing board. The purpose here is to give the architect a clear picture of what your library media center is now and what you envision it to be in the future. The more the architect understands about this, the more likely you will end up with a facility that works.

Prepare a Spatial Relationships Chart for the Architect

A spatial relationships chart, often called a bubble diagram, will show the various kinds of spaces required for your library media center, based on your program statement. The "bubbles" in the diagram will be proportionately sized to reflect space requirements and will show how the spaces must relate to one another. This chart must be in the hands of the architect well before any architectural plans have been committed to paper. If it is not, you might end up trying to fit your program into a given space, and this space will almost certainly not be enough!

Develop Budgets for Furnishings and Technology

Even though you will not yet have an exact inventory of furnishings and equipment needed for the new facility, you can, using your needs assessment, make reasonably accurate lists with estimated prices. Although it is not the most accurate method of estimating costs, you can calculate average costs based on the square footage your plan requires. (Obtain figures from other school librarians in your geographical area who have recently gone through building projects.) The extent to which you will be involved with establishing budgets will depend on local circumstances. You should have two separate budgets—one for furniture and one for computers and other equipment. In some cases, someone else in your school district will develop the furnishings and equipment budgets. Or these budgets may be developed later by the architect. In either case, try to have your opinions heard before the budgets are established. (In projects where a library is being expanded significantly, or where there is no existing library being replaced, an additional budget will be required for the collection of resources.) These budgets should be separate from the architectural design budget. If they are not, you may have less control over what is purchased. It is important to remember that libraries require specialized furniture and many items of equipment, and the costs will be higher than the costs of furnishing and equipping a classroom on a square-foot comparison basis.

Select an Architect

School librarians are rarely involved in the architect selection process, particularly if the library is part of a larger school building project. This is unfortunate because the selection of an architect will, to a very large extent, determine the overall success or failure of a new facility. Volunteer to help with the selection process. If you can be part of this process, be prepared. Ask prospective architects what experience they have designing schools and libraries in general and school libraries in particular. If they have never designed a library, tread with caution, but don't necessarily reject them solely on that basis. Inexperienced architects may be more inclined to solicit and take seriously your ideas. If they have library design experience, visit these libraries if you can, or at least ask the architect for pictures. Talk with staff at these libraries, and ask for opinions of the quality of the work and of the ease or difficulty of working with the architect. Ask yourself if you feel comfortable dealing with the architect. If an architect seems arrogant, threatened by your questions, or unwilling to understand your specific needs, that architect should not be hired.

Monitor the Development of the Architectural Plan

As the architect moves through the process of developing the architectural plan, you should be involved with every step related to the library. This is when the size and shape of the library space, as well as any division of spaces within the library itself, will be determined. Monitor its development to ensure the plan reflects, as closely as possible, the specifications made in your planning documents, in particular the bubble diagram. At this point in the process it is important to put in writing any recommended changes. When a change has been agreed to, be certain new plans are drawn that reflect the change. Remember this guiding principle: the earlier you request and establish a change in the design development process, the less expensive it will be.

Develop a Zone and Furniture Plan

At this point, the architect has been selected, plans have been developed and revised, and, eventually, a final architectural plan will be in place. While this is happening, you will benefit from learning some basics of architectural blueprint reading. You will also have been extensively involved in the development of the library media center portion of the architectural plan. Now it is time to zone the new library and make the furniture plan (see chapter 6).

Analyze the Furniture Plan

Before your furniture plan is finalized, you will want to analyze it in terms of design elements, colors and textures, traffic flow, accessibility, ergonomics, and maintenance. You will also want to be certain that acoustics, lighting, electrical, telephone, signage, security, and climate control have been adequately planned for. This is a crucial step, because once plans are finalized, making changes is very difficult.

Visit the Construction Site

Once plans are final and ground is broken for construction, you will have little to do with the actual building process. Nevertheless, this is a good time to buy or borrow a hard hat and, when permissible (following proper procedures, of course), make inspection visits to the site to monitor progress of the library. Frequently, changes must be made to plans once construction is under way, and no one may think to inform you. This is the time when what you have learned about reading blueprints will come in handy. If you see something that looks wrong, ask the architect.

Prepare Furniture Specifications and Obtain Samples

In most cases, furnishings will have to be specified and put out for bid before orders can be placed. This requires a detailed description of every item of furniture. Select possible vendors, those to whom you will submit the specifications for bids, and request samples of chairs, shelving, and tables. This step is often overlooked, but if you can take time to try out the furniture, you can help avoid the possibility of getting furniture that is not suitable.

Develop a Plan for Moving

If you are moving from an existing facility, you will need to make a plan for moving library materials and equipment to the new facility (see chapter 12).

Issue Bid Requests

Either the school's business office or, in some cases, the architectural firm will likely issue requests for bids. What you need to do is make sure the specifications for library furniture reflect your requirements.

Analyze Bids

The librarian is often overlooked in this phase of the project. Don't be! You want to be certain the vendors chosen can fulfill the requirements. You may also need to make the case that cheaper is not always better. Understand that it is not usually an absolute requirement of bidding procedures that the lowest bidder be selected.

Supervise Installation of Furnishings and Equipment

Be on-site when the furniture is delivered and installed. Check and double-check everything. Have the furniture plan in hand and make sure that placement is correct. If you leave this up to the installers, they may not follow the plan, regardless of what you've told them.

Direct the Move and Begin Occupancy

When the time comes for the actual move, having a written itinerary in hand will help the process go smoothly. Settling into a new facility is not something you can do in a day. Allow yourself time to prepare properly for beginning your program. You want to be able to function well and as fully as possible from the first day of opening.

Celebrate Your Success

After a long, difficult process, you finally have a new facility. Your diligence has paid off, and, even though you may not have a perfect library, because a perfect library most probably does not exist, you can be proud of what you have achieved. Some schools will organize an official opening ceremony. Just as it is best not to rush opening the doors, it is best to give yourself some time to settle in before planning any kind of open house.

2

Working Successfully with Key Players

The Art of Communication

Good design begins with honesty, asks tough questions, comes from collaboration and from trusting your intuition.

—Freeman Thomas

Don't be afraid to say what you think. Freeman Thomas, one of the hottest automobile designers, believes in the importance of being able to communicate your ideas. The design premise "form follows function," though sensible and seemingly simple, does not always govern library building projects. When it does not, the blame can often be placed on poor communication. Effective school library media center facility design is the result of much talking and listening, not just designing. This chapter explores working and communicating with architects, building committees, and other constituents. Your ability to communicate effectively throughout the building process will, to a large extent, determine the overall success of the project. Any librarian who fails to recognize this does so at his or her peril. If you can communicate skillfully, you will likely avoid many headaches and costly mistakes. At the very least, you should be able to prevent worst-case scenarios.

The Librarian's Role

The first step toward good communication may involve insisting that your ideas are heard. In response to an article in *School Library Journal*, a librarian writes, "Principals and district-office folks rarely bother to let the lowly librarian have such input! . . . I was never asked for my ideas."[1] Perhaps her attempts to serve on the building committee, or to at least be allowed to have meaningful dialogue with the architect, met with no success. On the other hand, all too often librarians wait to be asked, and, when we never are, we wonder why. A lot of "shoulds" are at work here: we think our opinions should be solicited and valued; we believe the architect should come and talk to us. In a perfect world perhaps this would happen, but in reality, we can't afford to wait. This is a time when assertiveness is called for, not meekness. There is too much at stake, so we must insist on being involved. The librarian who "was never asked" ended up with a library she described as

> a nightmare to try to teach in: . . . no place for bulletin boards, no blackboards, too few shelves that are too high, lights that take 25 minutes to come on, no outside windows, four doors that open onto the only space large enough for a

classroom, and people wandering through the teaching area without regard to what is going on.[2]

Developing Working Relationships

An unsuccessful working relationship with an architect, or poor communication with anyone involved in the planning, design, and construction processes, will also almost certainly lead to failures in your new library facility. Stories abound of libraries that for one reason or another are disasters, where the architecture or some design element interferes with proper functioning. Among the worst of these are stories of libraries that literally sank because the architect forgot to take into consideration the weight of the books. This is extreme, of course. Yet even a seemingly small architectural problem can amount to a major nuisance. For example, the failure to put a light switch at the library's entrance will cause staff members to feel their way around on dark mornings to turn on the lights.

Although we would like to blame the architect for any and all problems, most often the blame is shared by everyone. The solution is to build strong relationships with key players early in the process. Unfortunately, a library with the kinds of nightmarish problems just described costs as much to build as a well-designed, well-functioning library, and the students must cope with the inadequate facility for many years to come. You are the library professional and know best what you want from the facility. If you don't know what you want, you will have problems. It is your job to know what is needed, make yourself a key player, and effectively communicate your message.

The Building Committee

Your first contact may be with the planning team. The size and makeup of this committee will depend on the organizational structure of the school and the scope of the project. If your new library is part of a larger school building project, a building committee will be formed. In some situations, this committee will be responsible for all decisions. In others, there will be several subcommittees, each charged with a specific task. The building committee should represent all interested parties: administrators, teachers and librarians, staff members, school board members, parents, and students. Try, too, to include a representative of the custodial staff who can address maintenance issues that other committee members may fail to see.

As soon as possible, try to become a member of the building committee. How you accomplish this will depend to a great extent on the politics of your particular school. Waiting to be invited is not an effective approach. Ask to be on the committee, and justify your request. As a committee member, be responsible for keeping the entire school community informed about the library portion of the project. If you are not on the building committee, find a committee member who will keep you properly informed and who will present your written requests, ideas, and concerns to the full committee.

The Consultant

Although the hiring of library building consultants is not as common in school construction as it is in public and academic library construction, it is more prevalent than it once was. A good consultant will help you avoid costly mistakes and ease demands on your time and energy, which are probably already stretched to the limit. You may need to ask for help by requesting that a consultant be hired. Don't think that asking for help with the process reflects any inadequacies on your part. School librarians generally do not have training or experience in designing a library, nor should this be expected. Furthermore, designing a new library requires a great deal of time, and you already have a full-time job. Keep in mind that compared with other construction costs, consultants are inexpensive. And if your consultant helps you avoid even one mistake, you may well have saved more than the cost of her or his fees.

Ideally, a consultant is hired before the architect is hired and works with you until the end of the project. You can, of course, hire a consultant at any time or for specific parts of the process where you may need help the most. If you bring in a consultant too far into the process, however, it may be too late to correct mistakes that have already been made. Ideally, a consultant should work for you, not for the architect. You want the consultant's opinions to be independent of those of the architect.

A school may hire a consultant independently or request that the architect retain the services of a consultant on your behalf. Depending on your state's reimbursement guidelines for school construction, the cost of hiring a consultant may qualify for reimbursement. It is worth investigating this option.

How do you find a good consultant? Get recommendations from other school librarians, from lists your state association may have compiled, or from the building consultants list maintained online by the Library Administration and Management Association (LAMA). Because the requirements of a school library facility are different from those of a public or academic library, look for a consultant with school library facilities design experience as well as recent experience working in a school library. Before hiring a consultant, obtain references and check them. Because you will be working closely with the consultant, you want to hire someone with whom you can work easily.

The Architect

If the building committee selects the architect and if you are a member of that committee, you will be involved in this aspect of the process as well. If a separate committee is formed for architect selection, try to be on that committee; you may be able to help select an architect with whom you will have fewer difficulties down the road. If, however, you are not involved in the selection process, do what we librarians do so well—provide the selection committee with helpful information and a list of library-specific questions to ask.

Although it can be to your advantage to hire an architect experienced in designing school libraries, you should not necessarily dismiss out of hand an architect with no such experience. Often less-experienced architects are more amenable to soliciting and following your advice.

Once the architect is selected, determine who will have the authority to sign off on decisions. Try to establish yourself as the person who will communicate library-specific information to the architect. If you rely on someone else to do this, the danger of miscommunication looms. If for some reason you cannot speak directly to the architect, but must channel your information through a building committee or its representative, always put the information in writing. You want to avoid the situation in which the architect gets conflicting directions—one set of instructions from you and something completely different from someone else.

It is important to remember that an architect's time is limited. It is unlikely that you will have as much time as you would like to discuss the project with the architect. Plan carefully for meetings you do have so the time is well spent.

Communication Tips

Throughout the building process, compromises will be required between you, the architect, and other key players. You want to avoid conflict escalating to the point where further collaboration becomes difficult if not impossible. As a school librarian, you have lots of experience in human relations and communication skills. Put these to work. Don't abdicate your role in the process, but be a skilled negotiator and diplomat. Many times, architectural blunders are not solely the fault of the architect but are simply a result of miscommunication. Aim for relationships that are cordial and productive rather than adversarial.

Here are some points to remember:

Be a good listener. Keep an open mind to others' ideas.

Be consistent. Don't ask for lots of windows one week, and the next week say you want few or none. Know what you need and want in advance.

Be thorough. Don't overwhelm the architect with information, but give as much information as is relevant, including pictures of interiors that show features you particularly like.

Be timely. As soon as you identify a problem or concern, report it. The further into the process, the more costly changes become.

Be observant. If you've ever built or renovated a house, you know that construction errors are almost inevitable. If you see something that is wrong, or even if you only suspect it's wrong, report it.

Be appropriate. Don't ask about furniture specifics when the architect has just begun initial design concepts. Understand the process.

Be reasonable. Architects must work within budgets and conform to building codes. If you want a 12,000-square-foot library and the budget allows for only 6,000 square feet, you simply will not get what you want.

Be clear and concise. Architects cannot work with vagueness. Make certain the architect understands what is needed. You may not understand the architect's vocabulary, so don't assume the architect understands yours. For example, consider what the term "circulation" means to you. It means something quite different to an architect.

Be willing to compromise. If you're in a typical school district, you're building a Chevrolet, not a Cadillac. Set priorities and choose your battles, because you will not get everything you want. Your goal should be a facility that will allow for future change and growth.

Be assertive, but not aggressive. If you don't understand something, say so!

Be savvy. Learn to read architectural blueprints. Know at least the basics. Appendix A illustrates some commonly used architectural symbols. These symbols tend, however, to vary from architect to architect. When in doubt, ask the architect to clarify a symbol.

Remember, architects are not school librarians, and school librarians are not architects.

Perhaps the most important thing to recognize and remember is that planning a new library facility is a collaborative process. You must play a major role, but obviously you can't do it alone. Before anything happens, it is good to acknowledge this fact and to remember that you have no choice but to rely on the expertise of others. Equally important, remember that you and your school are the client, and the architect's responsibility is to meet your needs. The school is the boss. Most architects realize they need your expertise to provide them with proper focus, and they will willingly address your concerns and implement your suggestions. Some architects, however, may try to make you feel you are in no position to question them. Don't allow this to happen. Do not let yourself be intimidated! Stand your ground. You have a right to question and disagree. On the other hand, don't so stifle the architect's creativity that you end up with a library that is functional but dull and dreary. And do try to ask questions judiciously. You don't want to be someone the architect tries to avoid.

NOTES

1. "Librarians' Designs Disregarded," *School Library Journal* (April 1999): 8.
2. Ibid.

3

Planning Your Program

It's Never Too Soon!

James Conant, education administrator and former president of Harvard University, understood the importance of planning ahead. Designing a new or renovated school library facility requires deliberate, purposeful planning—planning that must begin far in advance. The success of a new facility depends to a large extent upon decisions made early in the process, decisions based on clearly articulated program considerations. A poorly designed school library is often the consequence of insufficient planning. Without a well-defined comprehensive program plan, you will end up with a facility where function follows form, where the program is limited by a dictated architectural design.

Obtaining a school library facility where design is ruled by the function of the program is a challenge. Architects bring design skills to the table; you bring the program definition. Getting these to mesh is often a frustrating process. Having a plan that articulates your program, its human activities, and attendant space requirements will help the architect understand the overall picture. And do keep in mind you are planning for tomorrow's program, not for today's.

Program planning, together with technology and space planning, results in the development of educational specifications. If the school library is part of a new school building project, the specifications for the library will be just one component of a larger document. State department of education requirements will often determine the exact format of the educational specifications document.

The educational specifications guide the design and construction project developed by the architect. Designing a school library is a new experience for many architects and school administrators. How well everyone in the design process understands the library program and how it functions within the school will affect the success of the design. Therefore, it is important that the program documents be as complete as possible and written in clear, unambiguous, and jargon-free language. A well-crafted plan articulates your program to others and identifies which aspects of the plan are essential and nonnegotiable and which aspects can be open to discussion and compromise. A good program plan has an added benefit: by effectively matching educational goals and objectives to be achieved by the school library media program with those established by the school, the program plan provides a tool for ongoing evaluation and a foundation for all future program decisions.

So, the design of the school library facility must be based on a set of beliefs: beliefs about students, the school itself, the educational process, the activity of learning, and the role of information in today's instructional process. An examination of these beliefs about schooling and the role of the school library in the teaching and learning process is a prerequisite for program planning. In today's schools, moreover, accountability is important; the library program must be based on evidence of what practices work, and the school library's contribution to learning and student achievement must be demonstrated.

Program planning begins with the belief that the school library media center of the future will serve a much broader educational role, and with questions that help you form a vision: Where do you want to be five years from now? What will students and teachers be doing in this new facility? What will the program offer students and teachers? Once these questions are answered, examine where your program is now and determine what is needed to realize this new vision of the program.

School libraries are in transition, and this process is affecting the design of our school library environments. School libraries have changed from places of resource ownership and storage to places where information is accessed, challenged, and created; from centers of curriculum support to extensions of the classroom; from places designed primarily for quiet, individual use to active learning environments. Resources in many formats and from worldwide locations are now available to students and teachers, making print collections less important for student reference work, particularly in middle and high school libraries. Much of the information that was formerly contained within school library walls is now accessible from locations beyond the confines of the library. Multiple uses occur simultaneously within school library walls. Teaching strategies encourage group collaboration and cooperation. Schedules are shifting from fixed to flexible, from equal periods to multipurpose blocks of time. Students are not the same learners they were ten years ago. Recent studies on how learning occurs and on what conditions best facilitate student learning demonstrate that the physical environment is an important component of quality schools.[1]

Our school library facilities must be planned to reflect these changes, to support the kinds of intellectual interaction new teaching strategies afford, and to incorporate "student as learner" characteristics.

Your program plan should include the following components:

1. *Vision statement.* A vision statement identifies who will benefit from the school library program and its services, what the benefits will be, what the results of these benefits are, and why these results are important.

2. *Mission statement.* A mission statement clarifies the purpose, business, and values of the school library by identifying the needs the school library program will address, explaining how these needs will be addressed, and delineating the principles or beliefs that guide the school librarian's work.

3. *Needs assessment.* A needs assessment identifies essential characteristics of quality school library programs and measures how well the present program is performing in terms of those characteristics. This assessment enables you to determine changes needed to better meet the instructional requirements of students and teachers.

4. *Program goals and measurable objectives.* This section of the plan includes program-oriented goals (describing the service and instructional components of the program) and organizational goals (describing the managerial and organizational components of the program). These are accompanied by measurable objectives that concretely define how goals will be achieved and include components for assessment. These goals and objectives detail how the mission of the school library program will be achieved.

5. *Program activities.* Written descriptions of the types of activities, the resources needed, and the number of students and staff members involved will help the architect understand the spaces required for the varied activities of the school library.

6. *A projection of future needs and growth.* A forecast identifies anticipated program or population changes that will require either more space or a different configuration of space: increased use of the library (particularly by classes and small groups); increased use of technology and digital resources; or more students needing small, quiet study spaces or spaces that are more teen and child friendly.

To properly define your program, you will need a solid knowledge of the national and state standards or guidelines as well as an understanding of the philosophy of your school. Many good resources are available in the professional literature to guide you through the program planning process (see Selected Readings).

As you embark on the planning process, keep the following points in mind:

Think of program planning in terms of defining a problem. Architects tend to think of building projects as solutions to problems.

Establish a bottom line. Decide what is negotiable and what is not.

Examine details. Don't take shortcuts.

Use your network of colleagues and friends. Bounce ideas off them to help process your thoughts.

Avoid being reactive. Focus on being proactive in articulating your program needs.

Challenge assumptions. This is your opportunity to be innovative.

Examine changes in the overall school landscape. For example, have classroom collections seriously diminished the school library collection, and should these be included in the library inventory for accountability? Is this a fad or a permanent situation? Where do students gather during the day to access their e-mail? Is this an appropriate school library service, and, if so, how is the traffic flow handled?

All this planning requires time. It is important to begin early so you can avoid planning in panic. No matter how you create the time to plan and be closely involved in the renovation or building project, it will be time well spent. Do not let what may be a once-in-a-lifetime opportunity slip through your fingers. The school library you help to design will exist for at least the next twenty-five years. This is a rare opportunity to make a significant difference in the lives of future students and teachers.

NOTE

1. Mark Schneider, *Do School Facilities Affect Academic Outcomes?* (Washington, DC: National Clearinghouse for Educational Facilities, November 2002), http://www.edfacilities.org/pubs/outcomes.pdf.

4

Planning for Technology
The Essential Ingredients

Effective planning requires a forward-thinking approach, and when it comes to planning for technology, looking forward rather than backward can make the difference between success and failure. When designing a new school library media center, it would be well worth thinking about how best to walk into the future.

Along with collaboration and leadership, technology is one of three basic components that "underlie the vision of library media programs presented in *Information Power: Building Partnerships for Learning.*"[1] In today's school library media center, technology is an essential ingredient. The school library needs to be the school's information hub, the place where students can find, use, and produce information in a variety of formats as well as explore ideas and pursue personal interests. The library media program must also be a full partner with other core subject matter areas in the development, implementation, and assessment of student learning objectives, and library media center technology is an important element of that partnership. When designing a twenty-first-century school library media center, technology warrants special attention in the facility planning process.

The extent of technology planning required in connection with designing a new or renovated school library facility will depend on two elements: (1) the technology plan your district and your school have developed (or not), and (2) the scope of the building project. If the scope calls for schoolwide technology planning, it is essential that the school librarian be an integral member of the technology planning and implementation team to ensure that library technology needs are met and that the plan is "aimed at supporting academic achievement rather than upon showy networks."[2]

The library media center is the place where students will use technology as a tool to explore a world of knowledge and to gather, evaluate, organize, and produce information; therefore, the library itself must be ready for a wide range of technologies. The need for network access and Internet connectivity in the library media center continues to grow. Most school libraries now use computer-based catalogs and circulation systems; software programs and Web resources are needed for personal discovery, student research, administrative work, development of instructional materials, and assessment of student learning.

GLOSSARY OF TECHNOLOGY TERMS

ACCESS POINT (AP) A device that connects wireless communication devices, such as a laptop, to the LAN and to wired devices such as printers. A WAP (wireless access point) usually provides Internet access to a laptop or PDA without requiring a connecting wire from the laptop to a network port on the wall.

ANALOG A variable electrical signal that is continuous in both time and amplitude. It differs from a digital signal in that small fluctuations in the signal are meaningful. Any information can be transmitted by an analog signal, including sound and data. Analog is the opposite of digital.

BACKBONE The top level of a computer network and the main network pathway for voice, video, or data traffic. The backbone connects all the other segments of a network.

BANDWIDTH A measure of data transmission rates when communicating over certain devices. In general, the wider the bandwidth, the greater the amount of information that can travel over the medium at one time.

BIT Short for binary digit, the smallest unit of computerized information. A single bit can hold only one of two values: 0 and 1. Meaningful information is created by combining consecutive bits into larger groups.

BPS (bits per second) The measure of the number of bits transmitted or processed in one second.

BYTE A byte is composed of eight consecutive bits that form a unit of data. It is a unit of storage measurement in computers regardless of the type of data (voice, video, or text). Amounts of memory are expressed in thousands (kilobytes per second, or Kbps), millions (megabytes per second, or Mbps), or billions (gigabytes per second, or Gbps). One kilobyte (KB)=1,024 bytes, one megabyte (MB)=1,048,576 bytes, and one gigabyte (GB)=1,024 megabytes.

CABLE PLANT All of the installed telecommunications wire and cabling needed for a complete and operational computer network system.

CATEGORY 5 CABLE (Cat 5) Computer network cabling that is made of four twisted pairs of copper wire. Cat 5 cabling supports computer frequencies up to 100 MHz and speeds up to 1,000 Mbps. Cable length is limited to a maximum of 90 meters.

CATEGORY 5E CABLE (Cat 5e) An enhanced version of Cat 5 cable that became available in 2001. Cat 5e is an excellent choice for use with Gigabit Ethernet (1000BASE-T).

COAXIAL CABLE A cable consisting of a center wire surrounded by insulation and a grounded shield of braided wire that minimizes electrical and radio frequency interference. Coaxial cable is used for cable television signal transmission.

The Challenge of Technology

Technology planning can be one of the greatest challenges of the planning process, and, for school librarians who are not technical wizards, it can be intimidating. Who among us can keep up with the fast and ever-changing pace of technology? When planning the requirements for technology in a new or renovated school library facility, the goal is a stable infrastructure that provides for today's needs and at the same time provides for technology changes and enhancements in a cost-effective manner for several years after the building project is completed. Although this may seem difficult at first, it is an achievable goal.

The challenge of planning for tomorrow's technology is evident when we consider that school buildings constructed as recently as ten years ago are largely unable to accommodate even the modest demands of today's technology. So what can you do? You try to apply today's best practices to the needs projected three to five years out. This will help you provide adequately for today and be ready to respond to future changes. We can be certain that technology will continue to develop at a dizzying pace, that information in electronic formats will become more and more pervasive, and that an ever-increasing number of students and teachers will be using more sophisticated and varied technologies. In terms of electrical sources, remember that even battery-powered laptops and handheld and other portable devices need electrical access to charge the batteries. Focusing on these certainties along with a vision of how technology may be incorporated into teaching and learning will result in a facility design that provides for technological change without a need for major structural enhancements and renovations. Furthermore, it is important for all members of the planning team to realize that because the library media center is a large and somewhat open space, and because that space will need to be reconfigured to accommodate new and increased use of technologies, it must be as flexible a space as possible.

As with all school construction and renovation projects, cost containment is important. Therefore, informed compromises will have to be made either in the size of the library media center facility or in the quality or quantity of materials and technology equipment purchased, or in both. The result of these sometimes uncomfortable trade-offs should be a library media center that has as many high-quality materials and as much technology equipment as you can reasonably afford now and at the same time allow for future growth and expanded use of technologies. Because resources are limited, it is important that the following questions guide your technology planning:

> What technologies will be used in the library media center, who will use them, and how will they be used?
>
> How is use likely to change over the next three to five years?

The complexity of planning for technology, as well as the need to contain costs, makes professional assistance particularly important. Try to enlist the help of a specialist, whether it be someone hired to work specifically on library technology planning or someone hired to provide overall school technology planning. At the very least, a technology specialist should be included on the architect's design team. Be aware that not all consultants are up-to-date on the latest technologies or on the most effective ways to reduce purchase costs when solutions are selected. Too many consultants simply specify hardware and software and move on to their next project. The best consultants are interested in building a consultative relationship, where the focus is not on the equipment but on how specific technology solutions can best help you achieve your goals and objectives. A good consultant will want to develop a long-term relationship that will assist and guide you not only today but for years to come as your technology needs and solutions change.

A Connectivity Primer

It is important for you to be considered an effective partner as you work with architects, contractors, vendors, and others who will be involved in planning technology for the library media center. To make informed decisions you should have a basic understanding of infrastructure issues relevant to educational technology. Some technical areas where a basic understanding may be helpful include: (1) local area network (LAN), metropolitan area network (MAN), and wide area network (WAN) infrastructure; (2) cabling and cable pathways; (3) wireless networking; (4) remote-access capability; and (5) video networks.

CONVERGENCE The coming together of two or more disparate technologies. Converging technologies refers to the transmission of voice, video, and data on the same network using the same cable plant and network devices.

CPU (central processing unit) The brain of the computer. The CPU is where most of the calculations take place, and it is the most important element of a computer.

DIGITAL A system based on discontinuous data or events. Computers are digital machines because at their most basic level they can only distinguish between two values, 0 and 1, or on and off. All the data that a computer processes, the visual information that a digital camera processes, and the sound that a compact disc processes must be encoded digitally, as a series of zeros and ones. Digital is the opposite of analog.

DISTANCE LEARNING A type of instruction in which students work at a remote location and use technology such as e-mail or videoconferencing to communicate with faculty or other students or both.

ETHERNET A common method of networking computers in a local area network (LAN) at rates of 100 Mbps (100BASE-T, or Fast Ethernet) and 1,000 Mbps (1000BASE-T, or Gigabit Ethernet). Ethernet is the most widely implemented LAN standard.

FIBER-OPTIC CABLE Cable constructed of thin transparent glass fibers for transmitting modulated light beams at high speeds and over long distances. Fiber-optic cable is used to transmit voice, video, and data.

FILE SERVER A computer on a network that manages stored files and acts as a shared network device. Any user on the network can be given rights to store and retrieve files on the file server.

FIREWALL A security device designed to prevent unauthorized or unwanted access to or from a private computer network.

GIGABIT (Gbps) When used to describe data storage, it refers to 1,024 megabits. When used to describe data transfer rates, it refers to 1 billion bits per second.

GIGABIT ETHERNET (1000BASE-T) A version of Ethernet that supports data transfer rates of 1 gigabit per second.

GIGABYTE (Gig, GB) In telecommunications, such as network speeds, gigabyte refers to 1 billion bytes. For computer memory sizes, gigabyte refers to 1,073,741,824 bytes.

HUB A central connection point for devices in a network. Hubs were commonly used to connect segments of a LAN. Today switches are more commonly used to connect LAN segments.

IDF (intermediate distribution frame) A cable rack used to interconnect and manage telecommunications wiring and networking equipment between the MDF and the end user's workstation and other network devices. Cables entering a building run through a centralized MDF, then through each individual IDF, and then on to specific workstations or other network devices. *See also* Telecommunications closet.

IP (Internet protocol) Standards that control communications on the Internet. IP-based videoconferencing uses an Internet connection.

LAN (local area network) A computer network that spans a relatively small area, usually confined to a single building or group of buildings. LANs connect workstations and personal computers so that users can access data and devices anywhere on the LAN.

LCD PROJECTOR (liquid crystal display projector) A device used for displaying video images or data to a group of people.

MAN (metropolitan area network) A data network designed for a town or city. A MAN is larger than a local area network but smaller than a wide area network and typically covers an area between 5 km (3.1 miles) and 50 km (31 miles) in diameter.

MDF (main distribution frame) A cable rack that interconnects the telecommunications wiring and networking equipment between itself and any number of IDFs and connects the private or public lines coming into a building with the internal network. *See also* Telecommunications closet.

NETWORK PROTOCOL A common set of rules and signals that computers on the network use to communicate. One of the most popular network protocols for LANs is called Ethernet.

PROTOCOL An agreed-upon format for transmitting data that must be followed for two computers or network devices to communicate.

REMOTE ACCESS The ability to connect and log on to a computer network from another location such as home. This usually requires a computer, a modem, and some remote-access software.

RF (radio frequency) That portion of the electromagnetic spectrum in which electromagnetic waves can be generated by alternating current fed to an antenna for transmission to another location.

STREAMING VIDEO A means of delivering video content over a computer network (LAN) in a way that allows the user to watch the video whenever she or he wants as it is being delivered, or "streamed," to the computer.

TELECOMMUNICATIONS CLOSET (TC) A room that houses all the equipment associated with phone, computer, and video network wiring systems. All telecommunications wiring is channeled through the TC. The larger the networks, the more TCs are needed: because of distance constraints in the type of wiring used, computers can only be a certain distance away from the TC. Networks that span multilevel buildings, such as schools, typically have a TC on each floor.

LANs, MANs, and WANs

Connectivity beyond the library media center and the school itself is one of the most important features of the computing environment. Several options exist to make these connections to the "inside" and "outside" world, and the options continue to improve. Local area networks (LANs), metropolitan area networks (MANs), and wide area networks (WANs) are networking topologies or infrastructures that connect individual computers to a building-based network, and building-based networks to each other and, in turn, to the Internet and the World Wide Web (WWW). The goal is to provide the most reliable and lowest-cost connectivity so that each individual desktop computer has efficient access to services, software, the Internet, and the World Wide Web, as required to support teaching and learning. The connectivity technology must be robust enough to connect hundreds of computers in a school and thousands of computers across a school district. For these larger applications, LANs, MANs, and WANs are most often used.

Cabling and Cable Pathways

There are three cable choices—copper, fiber-optic, or a combination of the two. Copper wire, sometimes called Ethernet cable, is less expensive than fiber-optic cable and, with the exception of some video-on-demand applications, is suitable for all of today's school applications. Cat 5 or Cat 5e (the "e" stands for enhanced) is currently the most cost-effective choice for school wiring applications.

There are two types of cable—riser and plenum. Riser cable provides vertical connectivity between floors; plenum cable is laid horizontally in plenum spaces—between the structural ceiling and the suspended ceiling, or under a raised floor. Plenum cable has a higher fire safety rating than riser cable. Although plenum cable is more expensive than riser cable, its increased safety makes it a responsible choice for all cable needs in schools.

The routing of cable to required locations is called a pathway. Pathways can be under the floor, in the walls, in support columns, in cable trays above a dropped ceiling, or connected to support structures with J hooks. The types of pathways will affect the functioning as well as the aesthetics of the library media center. Outlets determine where computers can be located and, obviously, should be planned so cables do not run across floors and doorway openings.

In a renovation, the options for locating cable drops and pathways are more limited than in new construction projects. In new construction, under-the-floor duct grid offers the most flexibility but is the most costly option and is rarely used in school applications. Locating pathways in walls and through columns is less expensive and is often preferred to floor mounts, where wet mops and student feet can render them useless. In renovations, surface raceway systems that are affixed to walls are frequently used, even though this is not the most aesthetic solution.

Enclosed channels for cable are called raceway systems, and they are available in single and duplex options. Duplex raceway allows for both network and electrical connections to run side by side. Keeping this in mind when planning the layout of the library will help to contain costs and maximize flexibility. If you plan to implement wireless LAN capabilities (discussed later) now or sometime in the future, electrical and data connections may need to be installed in the ceiling.

Wiring the building is expensive. Once the wire is in the walls it is not easy to make changes; therefore, it is essential that you plan what technology is needed, where in the library media center it will be used, and how many connections will be required.

Wireless Networking

The subject of wireless networking often sparks a major discussion when new and renovated facilities are planned. To wire or not is an important consideration, because if you decide to go all wireless, there is most likely no turning back—retrofitting costs would be substantial.

There are two types of wireless connectivity products—infrared and radio frequency (RF) systems. The RF type is the one most often used for school-based wireless access points (WAPs or APs)—the equipment is placed on a wall or ceiling to provide wireless network connectivity. And don't forget that wireless access points also require electrical power.

Wireless networking eliminates the need to connect a computer to the wall with a cable, which increases the flexibility of computer placement in difficult rooms and large open spaces. But wireless networks do not provide speeds comparable to wired networks, and relying solely on a wireless system in a school library environment is not sufficient.

What to do? In the library media center, the best solution may be to provide network wiring in the walls, hard wiring for desktop computers, and wireless access

UPS (uninterruptible power supply) A battery backup device that maintains a continuous supply of electrical power to essential network equipment and servers in the event of a power outage.

UTP (unshielded twisted pair) A common form of data cable in which two unshielded copper wires are twisted together for the purpose of canceling out electromagnetic interference. The lack of shielding around the wire pairs results in a high degree of flexibility and rugged durability. UTP cables are found in Ethernet networks and telephone systems.

VIDEO NETWORK A combination of video signal processing equipment and coaxial cable wiring that distributes video, including cable television channels and VCR and DVD content, from a central location to rooms and televisions throughout a building.

VIDEO OVER IP Using video processors and servers to deliver video content over the LAN.

VIDEOCONFERENCING A combination of voice and video telecommunications technologies that allows two or more people in two or more locations to talk with and see each other in real time using two-way video and audio transmissions simultaneously. This technology is also called video teleconferencing.

VIDEO-ON-DEMAND (VOD) A system that allows the user to select and watch video over a network as part of an interactive system that either "streams" the video, allowing viewing as the video is being downloaded, or "downloads" the video, bringing the program to the set-top box before viewing starts. All download and some streaming video-on-demand systems provide the user with a large subset of VCR functionality, such as pause, fast forward, fast rewind, etc.

WAN (wide area network) A computer network that connects several computers across a large geographic area. WANs are used to connect local area networks so that users and computers in one location can communicate with users and computers in other locations.

WIRELESS ACCESS POINT (WAP or AP) *See* Access point.

WIRELESS NETWORK (WLAN) The same as a LAN, which is the linking of two or more computers, but without using wires. WLAN is based on radio waves to enable communication between computing devices in a limited area with the ability to move around and still be connected to the network. In a WLAN, devices share a fixed pool of resources, so the more devices that connect to the WLAN, the lower the available bandwidth.

WIRING CLOSET *See* Telecommunications closet.

WORKSTATION Any computer connected to a LAN is referred to as a workstation.

for laptop computers that students either bring in from home or check out for use in the library media center. This decision will require considerable discussion involving all school population groups.

Remote-Access Capability

Remote access is the ability to access data files and software tools from a computer outside the school. Providing remote access to the library catalog and electronic library resources over the Internet makes possible a virtual library available even when the school library is closed, and this can be cost-effectively and securely accomplished using a browser-based application.

Video Networks

Distributing video signals throughout the school is another area that is rapidly evolving as the technology matures. Technology exists to support video distribution over your computer network and, in some applications, to make any computer connection a potential video distribution point. The library should be equipped for this type of video distribution.

Electrical Requirements

A new library facility must be able to accommodate all present and anticipated future electrical needs. Therefore, the electrical system design should accommodate cost-effective expansion. To assist the architect with electrical planning, you will need to know the electrical requirements for each piece of equipment you anticipate supporting. A rule of thumb is 5 amps per item and one 20-amp circuit for every three to four computers. Some types of equipment (copy machines, laminators, etc.) have higher power requirements and may require dedicated circuits. Be aware that fire safety codes in some states forbid surge protector multi-outlet extension cords and strip molding electrical outlets.

As with data drops, it is too costly to position electrical outlets throughout the library. Think carefully about current and future needs. Spaces that may not need electrical power today may need power at a later date. Sometimes electrical plans specify a certain number of outlets per square foot, but this type of generic plan may not be adequate or appropriate. Electrical outlets that are flush with the floor are often included in the design. Because hard-surface floors are washed and

waxed and carpets are shampooed, this is not always the best solution, although for certain power requirements it may be the only solution. All support columns should have electrical outlets. Locate outlets on all walls, even those that will initially be covered by wall shelving. If you will have wall-mounted television monitors and VCRs, remember to specify wall outlets in the appropriate locations. You should plan for electrical connection boxes above the ceiling tiles, as they may be needed in the future for network WAPs or ceiling-mounted monitors. You should also ensure that your library network is protected with surge protectors, an uninterruptible power supply (UPS), and an automatic backup.

Heating, Ventilating, and Air Conditioning (HVAC)

One aspect of library design that is often overlooked is air conditioning and climate control in areas with technology equipment. The school library often houses a network closet that requires air conditioning or ventilation to keep the temperature around 70 degrees. Computers generate heat, and a computer lab with thirty computers can raise the room temperature about 30 percent. Clearly, it is important to be aware of room conditions and climate control options in technology-rich areas.

Telephone and Fax

Depending on the number of staff and the size of the facility, the library should have at least two outside telephone lines with long-distance capability. One line should be dedicated for a fax machine. The second line will support library staff in the offices, the workroom, at the circulation and reference desk(s), and in library classrooms. A portable telephone is a good investment as it will allow you to move around the library media center while speaking on the phone. This capability can be invaluable when contacting technical support centers for computer and software application problems, which often involves being on hold for a considerable length of time.

Theft Prevention

A theft-prevention system will be required in most junior high or middle school and high school library media centers. Two basic types of theft-prevention systems are available—magnetic and radio frequency. It is important to clarify with the manufacturer any special requirements for placement of the system's components, especially if you choose a magnetic system. Distances between the system's components and the library's computers, copy machines, and metal objects (including metal studs in a wall) must be carefully planned to avoid any potential problems. Lighting fixtures can also affect the proper operation of some theft-prevention systems. Make certain the system you choose is appropriately placed in relation to other media center equipment and will function with whatever lighting is planned.

It is important to choose a theft-prevention system early in the planning process. The architect will need to know the specific placement requirements to allow for successful installation of the system's components. Electrical wiring for the theft-prevention system can be installed in several ways. In new construction, the cables can be buried in a raceway under the finished floor. This method is best in terms of both appearance and ease of maintenance and requires exact installation specifications. Alternative installation methods require routing the cables in a surface-mounted raceway or in an aluminum threshold on the floor's surface.

Radio Frequency Identification (RFID) is a recent technology introduced to manage library resources. It can provide both security and tracking of items but is expensive to install ($1.75–$2.00 per item), and, though reliable, it is as easily defeated as the more traditional RF and EM (electromagnetic) systems. It affords very quick reads of multiple items, speeding up returns by checking them in at the point of return without additional scanning, and makes self-checkout for the patron a bit easier. Some of the RFID literature, however, discusses concerns about patron privacy, and, for the small collections common in school libraries, RFID is an expensive and problematic alternative to more traditional automated circulation and inventory management practices. The American Library Association has adopted a Resolution on Radio Frequency Identification (RFID) Technology and Privacy Principles. This document is essential reading for anyone considering RFID technology.

Library Media Center Classroom

A library media center classroom should provide a flexible teaching environment that makes multiple seating configurations possible and has the means for present-ing information in a variety of ways. It includes computers with network access equal to the number of seats as well as peripheral devices such as a scanner, a printer, a document projector, a ceiling-mounted LCD projector with a ceiling-mounted sound system, and an interactive whiteboard (discussed later), all connected to the teacher's computer. The goal is to have the equipment connected so that all the teacher has to do is turn on the computer and LCD projector and everything works. The classroom should have electric power sufficient to support more equipment than will be initially installed. Electrical outlets should be located around the room, near the instruction area, and at all student tables. Controls for operating equipment should be conveniently located and simple to use.

Small-Group Study Rooms

Because the purpose of small-group rooms is to provide spaces that can function in multiple ways, it is important that they be spaces capable of supporting varied technologies. Students need to be able to select, combine, and produce information in the library media center and communicate their new knowledge in a variety of formats. Small-group rooms can effectively serve this purpose. Because such use will require capabilities for some multimedia production, you should plan for extra data and electrical outlets. Students using these rooms may need to recharge batteries for laptops and other personal listening and computing devices, so consider these power needs as well.

Videoconferencing and Distance Learning Classroom

A variety of distance learning designs are available. Some distance learning designs are based on using e-mail and are accessed by the learner at his or her convenience. Other distance learning designs use two-way interactive IP-based videoconferencing technology for face-to-face communication between the learner and instructor at a predetermined time. The objective is to have students and teachers communicate while physically located in different places. The technology needed for a videoconferencing/distance learning classroom varies and, as with all instructional facilities, should be determined by the kind of activities that will take place in the room.

The following equipment should be considered when planning a videoconference/distance learning classroom: digital video cameras with pan and tilt capability and monitors at the front and back of the room; an in-ceiling audio system; easy-to-use audio and video monitor controls; computers; printer; fax; telephone with conference call capability; document reader; DVD player (if one is not built into the computer); and overhead and LCD projectors. Wireless networking and power options for recharging laptop computers may be extremely effective in this setting.

The videoconferencing/distance learning classroom should be able to accommodate approximately fifteen to twenty students. To be most effective, the room should be carpeted for noise reduction and will require specially designed furniture that will allow everyone to see and be seen, and hear and be heard. Figure 4-1 shows one distance learning classroom design.

LCD Projectors and Interactive Whiteboards

A fixture in schools and library media centers today is the LCD projector, either on a mobile cart or mounted to the ceiling and often connected to a computer and an interactive whiteboard. The mobile LCD projector has the advantage of being easily moved to where it is needed. In a classroom setting, a ceiling-mounted LCD projector connected to a computer and an interactive whiteboard has the advantage of always being ready for use by simply turning on the projector and computer.

The sound available from an LCD projector is often not loud enough for everyone in the classroom to easily hear the audio content. If an instructional room is large and the projector is ceiling mounted or in a fixed location, an amplifier and speakers can also be installed in

Figure 4-1

Distance Learning Classroom

the ceiling. If you are using a mobile projector, purchase a set of powered speakers.

The standard LCD projector does not recognize and project closed captioning for the deaf or hard of hearing from videotapes or DVDs. You must specify this functionality when identifying projectors for purchase. If you need closed captioning for a projector that you already own, purchase a closed captioning decoder that will connect to the VCR or DVD player and communicate the closed caption content to the projector.

The interactive whiteboard can also be mobile or fixed. Each approach has advantages and disadvantages. If mobile, each time the whiteboard is moved the LCD projector will need to be set up, connected, calibrated (some interactive whiteboards automatically detect projected images and do not require calibration), and refocused. The fixed whiteboard has the same advantage as the fixed LCD projector: it is ready and easy to use. This is clearly an advantage for most teachers and appropriate for the library media classroom.

Mixed-Platform Challenges

Having Apple and Windows-based computers coexist in the same computing environment can create some technology management challenges. These challenges range from the desktop to the network and must be addressed by your instructional technology teachers.

Data-Driven Decision Making (D3M) and Data Warehousing

There is much talk in education today about data-driven decision making (D3M) and data warehousing. This phenomenon is a direct result of the federal No Child Left Behind (NCLB) Act passed in 2001. The school library network will need to access both types of data warehouses—transactional and informational. Library automation software is an example of a transactional data warehouse. Library instruction, where student performance is measured and analyzed, will draw on the informational warehouse, which includes many different types of statistics about students—demographics, test results, state standards, and so forth.

When school librarians are part of the assessment team and the library instructional program is integrated into the classroom curricula, school librarians become full partners in working to improve student achievement. Additionally, when library print and digital collections are significantly and effectively mapped to the school's curriculum and classroom instruction, the library media center becomes an indispensable, school-wide resource for improving student success.

Planning and Uncertainty

When we consider the potential of the library media center, it is important to consider not only current but also future technology trends. We can be fairly certain that wireless networks, digital video, voice recognition, interactive whiteboards, iPods, and equipment for distance learning will become common in K–12 instruction. It seems reasonable to expect accelerated use of instructional applications of technology.

At the same time, it is important not to be overly concerned with the uncertainties of the future. Ten experts who are members of the Library and Information Technology Association (LITA), a division of ALA, discussing the top technology trends, agreed that "one of the top trends in technology for libraries is you don't have to pay attention to all the trends."[3] This is good advice. What is important is to have the technology support the teaching and learning processes as transparently as possible. The focus should not be on the latest and greatest whiz-bang gadget but on what works seamlessly at the teachable moment. The effectiveness of technology is directly proportional to its transparency. Focusing too much on what might happen next may cause us to lose sight of what is important right now.

NOTES

1. American Association of School Librarians and Association for Educational Communications and Technology, *Information Power: Building Partnerships for Learning* (Chicago: American Library Association, 1998), 47.
2. David V. Loertscher, *Reinvent Your School's Library in the Age of Technology: A Guide for Principals and Superintendents* (San Jose, CA: Hi Willow Research and Publishing, 1998), 52.
3. Library and Information Technology Association, "Technology and Library Users: LITA Experts Identify Trends to Watch," February 1999, http://www.ala.org/ala/lita/litaresources/toptechtrends/midwinter1999.htm.

5

Planning Space Allocation
An Integrated Approach

We shape our buildings,
thereafter they shape us.
—Winston Churchill

Once you have carefully defined your program and identified your technology requirements, your next step is to examine space requirements and plan a facility with a shape and sufficient space for your program to be carried out efficiently and effectively. The words of the great English statesman and strategist Winston Churchill are worthy of your reflection; your goal now is to be involved in shaping the library facility. Once it is built, it will shape you, and only diligent and effective planning will help you to avoid adverse consequences. In this planning phase you identify: the kinds of spaces needed; what size these spaces should be; how the spaces must relate to each other; and the furniture, equipment, physical, environmental, and communications requirements for each space. You will also determine the desired collection size and seating requirements. If the library facility is part of an overall school building project, you will also want to address the location of the library within the school building as well as the number of entrances.

Initial Considerations

The lack of space in school libraries continues to be one of the biggest, if not the biggest, facilities-related complaint among school librarians. Because every square foot of a new building adds to the total cost, getting the space you want for the new school library facility will be one of the most difficult battles you will fight. No matter how hard you try, no matter how convincing your arguments, you will inevitably end up with less space than you believe you need. National guidelines for spaces in school libraries do not exist. This is not surprising, because every school has different requirements, and every school library program is unique. It is impossible to establish space guidelines that will be appropriate for every school. Most states have space guidelines for new school construction. These guidelines, however, are very often inadequate: they are based on an educational model that is no longer appropriate, and many of them were developed before the widespread use of technologies and digital resources began. Nevertheless, they are frequently adhered to religiously. Familiarize yourself with your state guidelines, and distinguish between recommended and minimum guidelines, which are often, albeit incorrectly, used synonymously. You may need to demonstrate why guidelines must be exceeded. Some architects as well as some school administrators believe that school libraries can be smaller than they were in the past, because print materials are being replaced by digital resources. This logic is flawed. Strong book collections remain a vital component of all school libraries. And when books are replaced by digital resources, the equipment needed to access these resources must be provided; this equipment requires considerable space. Furthermore, the complexity of finding quality information from digital media makes the need for library instructional space—space to instruct students and teachers—more important than ever.

With the shift to resource-based instruction, flexible scheduling of library media centers, and the need to accommodate both small- and large-group learning activities, school libraries must now accommodate a wider variety of groupings as more students use the facility. Gone are the days when a school library was considered sufficient if it could accommodate one class. Consider the Robin Hood Foundation's rationale for funding the transformation of school libraries in the New York City school system: "By investing in only 5 percent of a school's real estate—what Robin Hood estimates a library constitutes—it has an impact on 100 percent of the students."[1]

When the educational specifications are being developed, it is important to state how much space is needed to facilitate an effective, dynamic library program, one that truly enhances student learning. However, priorities must also be established, because financial constraints will make compromises necessary. By specifying optimum space requirements at the beginning, you will avoid the sudden realization, well into the building-design process, that the envisioned program will not fit! At that point, it will simply be too late.

Location of the Library

When a new school building is planned, the location of the library should be discussed and recommendations given to the architect. The library should be easily accessible from all learning areas of the school. Often this means placing the library in a central location. It should also be located away from noisy areas (the cafeteria, the gymnasium, and music rooms). Location on the ground floor is preferred (and is less expensive because of load-bearing requirements for shelving); if not on the ground floor, the library must have reinforced floors and be near an elevator. Location near a building entrance with access to restrooms will allow for extended use of the library during nonschool hours and will facilitate delivery of materials and equipment. Finally, specify a library location or a building design that will allow for cost-effective future growth and expansion.

Library Entrances

Building codes will govern entrances and exits. Required emergency exits can be designed as exits only: locked to deny access from outside the library and equipped with alarms if opened from inside the library.

Scrutinize the reasons for planning more than one main entrance. Multiple entrances make supervision more difficult. And if your plans include a theft-detection system, remember that you will need to equip each entrance, with the attendant costs of equipment and construction requirements.

Functional Areas

School libraries have always had basic space requirements: a circulation and service area, space to house the collection of resources, space for independent reading and study, storage space, storytelling areas in elementary school libraries, and work spaces for library staff. With the shift to digital media and changes in pedagogy, and the broadening of the role of the school library media program, new functional areas in the school library are needed. Sadly, too many new school libraries look much the same as school libraries designed in the 1960s. Yes, computers can now be found in our school libraries, but merely adding computers to the outmoded school library model does not transform it into a twenty-first-century facility. Too often the basic school library layout consists of a sea of tables (usually for six to eight students) and rows and rows of book stacks. This is yesterday's model, and it is no longer appropriate. The failure to address the functional complexities of today's school libraries could be considered malpractice: it is a waste of money and an injustice to students.

In order for the school library media center to function both as the school's hub for information technologies and information literacy instruction and as the place to go for ideas, perspectives, insights, knowledge, and learning, new spaces must be provided—spaces where digital media are accessed and created; where instruction occurs; where multimedia projects are produced; where various-sized groups can meet simultaneously and work without distractions; where school library media specialists can work with teachers to plan, conduct, and evaluate learning activities that incorporate information literacy competencies; and where student work can be exhibited. The importance of the library media center as a social setting for students must also be considered. Additional space requirements will vary depending on the school's educational goals and objectives.

Appendix B lists spaces most commonly found in school libraries, special requirements and adjacencies, and suggested square-foot allocations. This information will help you get started, but a lot of homework will be needed on your part. There is no simple, clear-cut formula for calculating space needs, no single solution that is right for every situation. The size of each space must be based on exactly what needs to happen in that space, and this will vary from school to school.

Three factors will greatly influence the overall space needed for the school library facility: the size of the print collection, the desired seating capacity, and requirements for the use of technologies.

The Print Collection

Predictions that books are the technology of the past have yet to come to fruition. Although it is true that digital resources have replaced and continue to replace many print resources, books will likely remain an important part of school library collections for the foreseeable future. Quality literature collections are needed for reading enrichment in all our school libraries. On the other hand, print collections to support school curricula will likely either remain static or shrink as we rely more heavily on (and students demand) digital information, and nonfiction collections may one day be obsolete.

Many states and accreditation agencies still use number of volumes as a means of evaluating the quality of school library media centers. The time for the school library community to address this issue in a meaningful way is long overdue. Few would deny that the emphasis must be placed on quality rather than quantity (to that end many guidelines now call for an evaluation of currency as well as volume count), and when collections

are evaluated, the availability and quality of media in all formats must be considered.

The book collections we do maintain must be relevant—that is, what is really needed in terms of the curriculum. Often books are still the most appropriate media, and it is imperative that school librarians and classroom teachers not overemphasize the role of technology, but teach students the importance of using books in tandem with digital media.

Instead of adhering religiously to any existing state standards that emphasize quantity, each institution needs to address and attempt to arrive at a consensus of what is an appropriate print collection size, taking into consideration the availability of quality digital media. There is no "one size fits all" solution, no definitive answer. Keep in mind that using Internet resources for curriculum-related work requires pulling together bits and pieces of data and forming a more holistic look at or approach to the information that will coalesce into knowledge and wisdom. This is time-consuming and, at the moment, inefficient as well as often ineffective. But also consider the viewpoint of Jamie McKenzie, a former superintendent, principal, school librarian, and teacher, that print collections no longer need to "offer comprehensive information on all topics. In times of scarce funding, we avoid information redundancy."[2]

As you wrestle with the appropriate size for your print collection, consider the fact that you have far less control over digital resources. Their content is determined by someone other than you, and their availability cannot be considered as permanent as books. It has been estimated that "the average life of a web page is 75 days."[3]

Once you have determined the desired collection size, you need to estimate the square footage required to accommodate that collection. The amount of space will depend on two variables: the width of aisles between stacks and shelving unit height. With an aisle width of 36 inches (the minimum ADA requirement), based on a standard 36-inch shelving unit, a 10-inch-deep single shelving unit requires 8.75 square feet; a 12-inch-deep unit requires 9.40 square feet. Increasing the aisle width to 42 inches, these figures change to 9.70 and 10.30 square feet, respectively. For double-faced shelving units, these figures are multiplied by two.[4] (See figure 5-1.) Thus, a high school library with a collection of 20,000 volumes, using 10-inch-deep shelving units with five shelves per unit (thirty books per shelf) and aisles 42 inches apart, would need a total of 1,300 square feet to house the general book collection.

Aisle width of 36 inches	Square feet required
10-inch single-faced shelf	8.75
12-inch single-faced shelf	9.40
10-inch double-faced shelf	17.50
12-inch double-faced shelf	18.80
Aisle width of 42 inches	**Square feet required**
10-inch single-faced shelf	9.70
12-inch single-faced shelf	10.30
10-inch double-faced shelf	19.40
12-inch double-faced shelf	20.60

Figure 5-1

Calculating Book Collection Space Needs: Space Required per 36-inch Shelving Unit

The example just given is a simple calculation. Actual needs will vary, because you will most likely use a variety of shelf heights and depths. And you may want to assume fewer than thirty books per shelf, or more than thirty for a picture book collection in an elementary school library (see shelving capacity estimates in appendix D). Another method sometimes used to determine square footage requirements for shelving is to allow one square foot for every ten books. In the preceding example, this formula would indicate a requirement of 2,000 square feet.

Seating Capacity

Recommendations for seating capacity of a school library range from 12 to 30 percent of student enrollment. The program and staffing should determine the seating capacity requirements. Some programs will require the library to accommodate more students at any one time. If present program requirements for seating are at the minimum, consider that changes in program or enrollment may increase these needs in the future. Try to allow some room for growth, or at least for the pos-

sibility of future expansion. As a minimum, an elementary school library should be able to accommodate at least one and a half classes, a junior high/middle school library at least two classes, and a high school library at least three classes simultaneously.

The size of the library staff should also be considered when planning the overall size of the facility. If the school library is understaffed, with no likelihood of an increase in the foreseeable future, it would be folly to build a 10,000-square-foot library with seating for 150 students. One person could never supervise it!

Technology Requirements

The requirements for technology that you have defined—hardware and software requirements, the technologies that will be used, how they will be used, and who will be using them—are the technology issues that relate specifically to space planning. Do not make the mistake of considering only the number of computers and printers you will have in the library. Technology requires additional space—and the amount can be substantial—that one may easily fail to consider: network and wiring closets to support the technology; storage space for equipment such as laptops, laptop storage/recharging carts, and video and digital cameras; spaces where students can recharge laptops and handheld devices; additional office space that may be needed for instructional technology staff; and additional space for mechanical systems necessitated by increased electrical and air conditioning demands.

You must also consider the space requirements for a computer workstation, which differ from the space requirements for a general reading and study seat. Depending on the table size, a general reading and study seat (including the area around it required for using it) will require from 15 to 30 square feet. A computer workstation will require from 20 to as much as 60 square feet depending on the type of use—short-term, long-term, individual, group (two or more), and so forth. Keep in mind that although computer hardware does not take up as much space as it once did, a workstation still must accommodate the hardware and peripherals, with room left over for print materials and a writing surface; the commonly specified 30-inch-wide workstation table is simply not adequate for most school library applications. Be meticulously thorough when defining how and where computers and other information devices will be used. Some of the questions you need to answer to calculate space needs include the following:

> Will you have dedicated public access catalog stations (PACs), and, if so, how many? Will they be stand-up stations, sit-down stations, or a combination? Will they be located in one area or distributed throughout the library?

> How many computer workstations will be for group work, and what sizes will these groups be?

> Where will students use laptops they bring from home? Will they use study tables, comfortable chairs with laptop tablets, or a combination?

Finally, you must consider both instructional needs and information production needs. Library classrooms, virtual learning spaces for videoconferencing and distance learning, and multimedia production spaces—space needs that will in all likelihood increase in the future—will quickly add substantial amounts to your total space requirements. Meaningful discussions, thorough needs assessments, and careful planning are essential.

Changing technology makes space planning difficult. But we can be quite certain that the demand for information devices of all types, and the connectivity of those devices, will continue to increase. Don't think today. Think future.

Descriptive Specifications

Once you have identified the types of spaces and determined the square footage requirements for each space, you need to prepare descriptive specifications for each area. (Appendix C shows an example of an area data sheet for an office/workroom.) In addition to identifying the space and listing the required space allocation, the specifications should include the following:

> A description of the activities that will take place in the area, who will use it, and how many persons will use it at any given time.

> Identification and quantification of any resources the area will have.

> A list of furniture and equipment required for the area, and the number and approximate dimensions of each item. (Be certain to include special items, such as built-in storage.)

> Communication requirements: electricity, telephone, and data.

> Special lighting, acoustical, and temperature/humidity requirements.

> Any other special requirements (for example, glass panels in office and workroom doors and walls, floor treatments, window treatments, and sinks).

Spatial Relationships Diagram

To clearly illustrate proper relationships of areas, a spatial relationships diagram (sometimes called an adjacency diagram or bubble diagram) should be prepared. The bubble diagram will show both desired adjacencies and proportionate sizes of individual areas in relation to the whole. Use circles (or rectangles) to show the various spaces. Circles that touch one another indicate the need for immediate adjacency. Circles that overlap indicate areas that flow from one into the other and are not separated by walls. Circles that do not touch indicate the need for corridors between the areas. Figure 5-2 shows an example of a bubble diagram.

A final note about library facility space: shapes that are as nearly square as possible are easier to lay out effectively and easier to supervise. Include this request with your educational specifications.

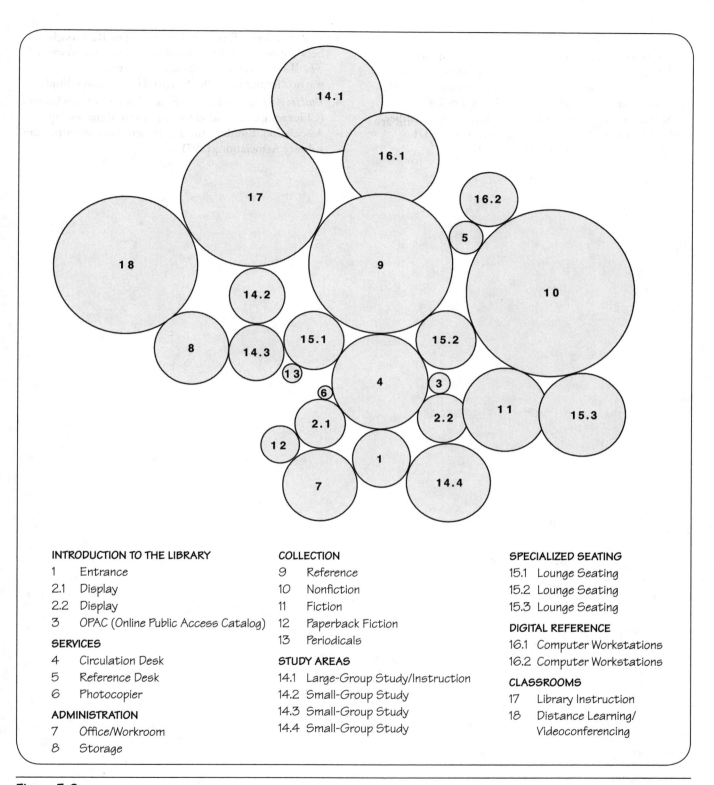

INTRODUCTION TO THE LIBRARY
1   Entrance
2.1   Display
2.2   Display
3   OPAC (Online Public Access Catalog)

SERVICES
4   Circulation Desk
5   Reference Desk
6   Photocopier

ADMINISTRATION
7   Office/Workroom
8   Storage

COLLECTION
9   Reference
10   Nonfiction
11   Fiction
12   Paperback Fiction
13   Periodicals

STUDY AREAS
14.1   Large-Group Study/Instruction
14.2   Small-Group Study
14.3   Small-Group Study
14.4   Small-Group Study

SPECIALIZED SEATING
15.1   Lounge Seating
15.2   Lounge Seating
15.3   Lounge Seating

DIGITAL REFERENCE
16.1   Computer Workstations
16.2   Computer Workstations

CLASSROOMS
17   Library Instruction
18   Distance Learning/
       Videoconferencing

Figure 5-2

Bubble Diagram for a High School Library

NOTES

1. Evantheia Schibsted, "Way Beyond Fuddy-Duddy," *Edutopia* (October 2005), http://www.edutopia.org/magazine/ed1article.php?id=art_1354&issue=oct_05#.

2. Jamie McKenzie, "The Techno-Savvy, Book-Rich Media Center," *Library Media Connection* (November/December 2003), http://www.linworth.com/PDF/LMC_NovDec_MKenzieFeat_lo.pdf.

3. A. B. Credaro, "Research Findings: The Relationship between School Libraries and Academic Achievement," *The Warrior Librarian* (2002), http://www.warriorlibrarian.com/RESEARCH/libresearch.html.

4. *Building Blocks for Library Space: Functional Guidelines* (Chicago: Library Administration and Management Association, Building and Equipment Section, American Library Association, 1995), 6.

6

Creating a Functional Interior
Zone and Furniture Plans

Design is a plan for arranging elements in such a way as best to accomplish a particular purpose.
—Charles Eames

Think purpose. You have now defined your program, determined present and projected requirements, and identified the types and sizes of individual spaces, and the architect has presented a general design defining the space the new library facility will occupy. How do you arrange the spaces you have identified? Charles Eames, the American designer and architect, viewed design as a means to solve a problem. As you begin one of the most critical phases of library design—creating a zone plan and a furniture plan—the problem you need to solve is how to arrange spaces and furniture in a way that will enable you to carry out your program in the most effective way possible. This phase should occur concurrently with the architectural design process. Certain elements of the architectural design needed for the final construction documents will be determined by the furniture plan: where the stacks are placed will determine floor-loading requirements, placement of technology and electrical equipment will determine electrical and data requirements, and furniture placement will determine lighting needs and placement.

Zone Plans

Making a zone plan involves reconfiguring the bubble diagram to fit the library's footprint, the space defined by the architectural plan. The bubble diagram shows spaces and adjacencies, and the zone plan should reflect these spaces and adjacencies as much as possible. Far too often the zone plan is skipped; the plan moves directly from the bubble diagram to the furniture plan. Preparing a zone plan is well worth the effort—it is an essential step in the process for creating efficient traffic patterns, and it makes planning the layout of furniture much easier.

Creating the Zone Plan

To begin the zone plan, take the total square footage of the new library and allocate the square footage for each space or zone. Ideally, you will have been given enough space to adequately accommodate all the program activities you want in the new library. In most cases, however, the space requirements originally requested will have been scaled down. If the overall size of the new library is substantially smaller than what was requested, some spaces may need to be eliminated altogether. The reality of school library building projects reflects the reality of school funding issues: there is never enough money, and, as a result, there is often not enough space. And you must be realistic when planning interior space. A given amount of space will accommodate only so much furniture, equipment, and activity.

Begin with the architectural drawings of the proposed library. Be sure that the drawings reflect the latest agreed-upon space. Then make a list of each defined zone within the library and the square-foot size of each zone. Cut out shapes in the same scale as the architectural drawing for each zone. Using the bubble diagram, begin arranging these zone shapes on the library plan. Keep in mind what doesn't work in your present facility and what doesn't work in other libraries you've visited, and try to eliminate those problems. Cut the shapes as needed so each zone fits into the plan, but use all the shape so each zone will reflect the correct amount of space. When the entire library is laid out this way, you can outline and label each space. Figure 6-1 shows an example of the zone plan developed for a high school library based on the bubble diagram shown in figure 5-2.

The next step is to indicate projected traffic flow patterns. Don't neglect this aspect of planning. A library should not be a maze, which it can be if traffic flow patterns are not carefully planned and delineated. Imagine yourself walking into the library, and draw lines and arrows indicating where library users and staff members will need to walk in order to move between zones. It may be useful to think of these as the streets or pathways within the library. Try to plan the flow of traffic in a way that is both obvious and efficient. Keep it simple; for a library to work well, it must be easy for the user to navigate. Because space in school libraries is often at a premium, the temptation is to utilize every square foot of floor area for furniture. Leaving open areas seems like an extravagant waste of space. However, the way a library functions is very important, and you don't want users running into obstacles at every turn. You also want the library to be inviting, and clutter and crowding are the antithesis of an inviting environment.

Traffic should flow along perimeters of zones, not through them. Do not, for example, create a main traffic lane directly through an area that will be used for instruction or through the center of the reference collection, where students need relatively undisturbed space. Pay particular attention to areas that class groups will walk through to reach group study spaces. The importance of planning for these traffic lanes will become apparent once you begin the furniture plan, as these areas must be free of obstructions.

When you think you are satisfied with the zone plan, look at it frequently for several days, trying to imagine working in and using these spaces. Get opinions from library staff, teachers, and students, and refine the plan to reflect any improvements.

A High School Library Zone Plan

Two versions of a zone plan for a new high school library are shown in figure 6-2. The shape of this library makes good zone planning difficult, but when a consultant was hired to assist with the planning process, it was too late to make any major size or shape changes. Because the architect placed the circulation area in the space connecting the two wings, supervision of the library would be extremely difficult. With two entrances, however, there were few options to consider. Two circulation areas could have been planned, one for each entrance, but the library would not be sufficiently staffed to make that option viable. The consultant recommended eliminating one entrance and locating a single entrance where the architect had placed the audiovisual storage room. The television and radio, large-group instruction, and teacher library areas were then grouped and placed in the left wing. Library staff members' ability to supervise these areas was less important, because these enclosed spaces would be used either by staff or by students with teacher supervision. The circulation area was placed near the entrance, but far enough into the library to make supervision of all student areas possible.

Furniture Plans

Developing a furniture plan is often given far too little attention, with too little thought going into how the facility must function. The result in many cases is little more than a haphazard arrangement of furniture. This is one reason many school libraries are unsatisfactory. Often, too, school libraries appear to have been designed with a concerted effort to make them as neutral and unexciting as possible. Users of this kind of environment may feel bored and develop negative attitudes toward the library.

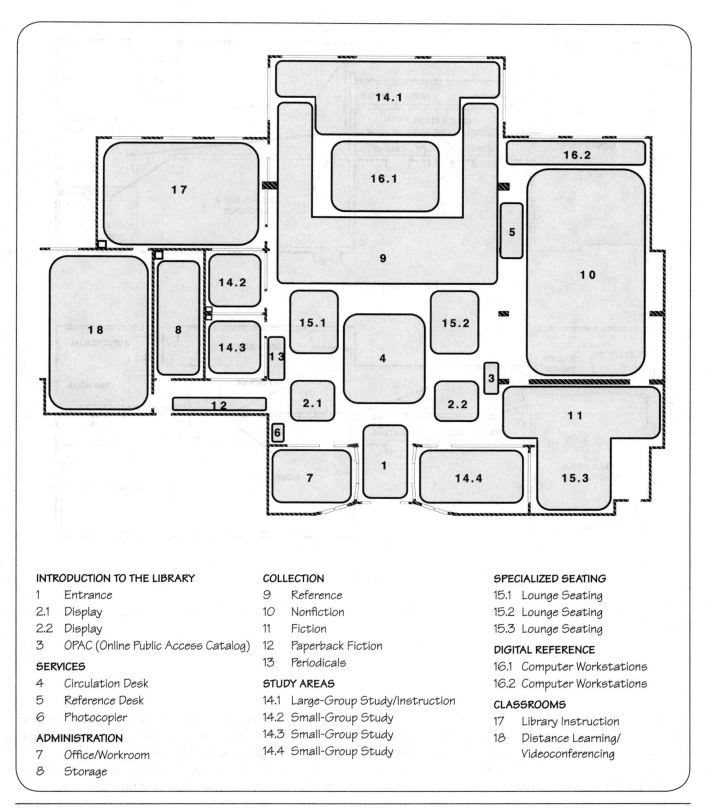

INTRODUCTION TO THE LIBRARY
1 Entrance
2.1 Display
2.2 Display
3 OPAC (Online Public Access Catalog)

SERVICES
4 Circulation Desk
5 Reference Desk
6 Photocopier

ADMINISTRATION
7 Office/Workroom
8 Storage

COLLECTION
9 Reference
10 Nonfiction
11 Fiction
12 Paperback Fiction
13 Periodicals

STUDY AREAS
14.1 Large-Group Study/Instruction
14.2 Small-Group Study
14.3 Small-Group Study
14.4 Small-Group Study

SPECIALIZED SEATING
15.1 Lounge Seating
15.2 Lounge Seating
15.3 Lounge Seating

DIGITAL REFERENCE
16.1 Computer Workstations
16.2 Computer Workstations

CLASSROOMS
17 Library Instruction
18 Distance Learning/
     Videoconferencing

Figure 6-1
Zone Plan for a High School Library

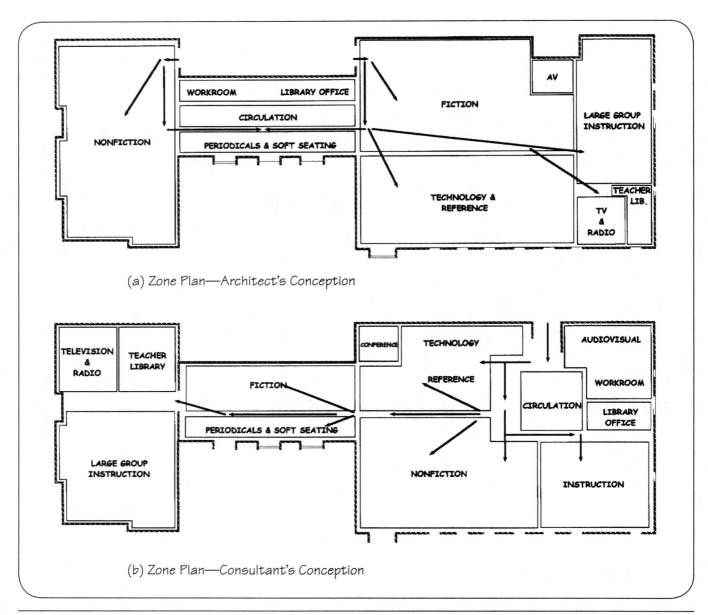

(a) Zone Plan—Architect's Conception

(b) Zone Plan—Consultant's Conception

Figure 6-2
Development of a Zone Plan for a High School Library

Many furniture plans proposed for school library facilities are boringly similar: rows of stacks and a sea of tables (which users often must walk through to reach the stacks). Unfortunately, planners often fail to recognize the distinct difference between school libraries and other types of libraries. A library model, probably designed for an academic institution, provides the basis for a furniture plan for a school library. The results are unsuitable. Also, too often new school libraries reflect outdated values and fail to accommodate twenty-first-century changes in school library programs.

The professional literature lacks information about the importance of a good furniture plan and how to successfully develop one. You can find numerous examples of library layouts, but the fact that a layout has been published does not necessarily mean it is a good example. Even award-winning examples, or examples someone believes to be exemplary, are often poor examples of good school library facility design. Looking at examples of layouts is useful, but it is not enough. Each library is unique, and what works for one school library may not work at all for another. The program must be the key consideration.

The goal of developing a furniture plan is to place all the required furniture and equipment into the zone plan in such a way that the overall layout, in addition to being user-friendly, convenient for users, and efficient for staff, will meet all criteria of the educational specifications. Making a furniture plan for a new library is not easy. The task requires the ability to visualize what a furnished space will look like, and many people, school librarians included, find this difficult. (This is where a three-dimensional rendering from a CAD, or computer-assisted design, program can be of enormous help.) In addition, you will need skills in interior design, lots of experience, and, most of all, common sense. Of all the phases of the library design process, this is the one where it is wise not to struggle alone, but to get some type of professional assistance, preferably from someone who understands children and adolescents and who has experience with twenty-first-century school library programs.

How your library is laid out will largely determine how well the new facility will work. And remember, no matter how much flexibility you may have achieved, once library furniture is installed, it is not easily moved; anyone who has had to move stacks can vouch for that. Some changes may need to be made after initial installation, but it is far better if such adjustments are minor. Careful advance planning is critical.

If possible, hire a consultant who has designed furniture layouts for school library facilities. If you can't afford this kind of assistance, try at least to have a consultant critique the layout you do yourself. You can also ask other school librarians to look at your plan and provide comments and suggestions. Some furniture vendors will tempt you with offers of free layout services. Such a layout provided by a vendor can be very useful, but be wary: you don't yet want to commit to a particular furniture vendor, and, because people with no school library experience sometimes design these layouts, the quality varies. Occasionally, vendor layouts are designed to sell a maximum amount of furniture. These plans can, however, provide a starting point.

Sometimes the architect will create a furniture layout. Unless the architect has considerable experience designing school libraries, it is essential to scrutinize an architect-developed furniture plan with a critical eye. Many furniture plans created by architects, although appropriate for public or academic libraries, are not appropriate for school libraries. Some architects will hire a library consultant or an interior designer experienced in institutional design to assist with the development of a furniture plan. In this case, it may well be good. The bottom line, however, is that no one is likely to develop a plan to fit your exact specifications unless you are involved.

No matter what kind of assistance you receive, don't abdicate your role in the process. Designing a successful furniture plan requires knowing how students will use the library, and you are in the best position to know this. View everything critically and meticulously, ask questions, and assume nothing. Above all, be willing to challenge tradition and convention. Although there may be great value in some time-honored traditions, when it comes to planning school library facilities, tradition should be rigorously questioned. The so-called traditional school library, designed for education in an era long since passed, is simply not appropriate for the strong and vibrant school library programs that need to exist in schools today.

Items in the Plan

To begin a furniture plan, make a list of each item of furniture for each zone, including the quantities needed and the depth and width dimensions. For some items (tables, for example), it is best to list optional sizes. This is only a working list, and it will be revised frequently.

SHELVING

Although it is one of the most difficult parts of the furniture plan, it is best to begin the layout with shelving. The number of shelving units will be determined by the print collection size specified in the planning documents. The height of the shelving units will determine the number of units needed and ultimately the amount of floor space required (see appendix D for general information on shelving). If space is tight, you may need to consider taller shelves, but you can begin planning with optimal shelf heights.

The Americans with Disabilities Act (ADA) requirements will determine some features of the shelving layout. (Chapter 10 covers this information in more detail.) ADA recommends 42 inches between shelving units, and it is wise to use this recommendation when space permits; 36 inches between units is the legal minimum.

Poorly arranged shelving in libraries can create major problems. Many shelving plans simply try to maximize storage. The result may be increased book capacity, but will likely also be a hodgepodge that is confusing to the user. Shelf capacity should be balanced with functionality, and sometimes less is indeed more. It doesn't do much good to have a wonderfully large collection if it is housed in an overly crowded space that is unpleasant to use. Such a collection may not be used much, because no one will want to be in the library. The shelving arrangement should organize the collection into well-defined areas for fiction, nonfiction, reference, and special items. The user should be able to locate the individual areas easily. Consider the flow of the collection: within each area, materials should be logically arranged to enable the user to move effortlessly through the collection to locate items.

Architects are sometimes asked to limit the number of windows in the library or to plan windows that will allow shelving below them, often in an effort to cram in as many shelves as possible. When space is limited, this may be unavoidable (but keep in mind the height of the students). Still, don't underestimate the advantage of having some windows to allow for natural light and ventilation or to provide for interesting outside views. It is also worth setting aside some unfurnished wall space for library displays and exhibitions of student artwork.

To allow for maximum flexibility, most school libraries are designed with public areas as one large space. Yet it is often desirable to create small areas within the library, areas with a feeling of being separate. Such areas can be created by using shelving as pseudo walls.

Another important consideration when planning the shelving layout is supervision. Stacks, especially those higher than 42 inches, should not be positioned in a way that obstructs visual control of the aisles; this is a critical safety issue. The shelving layout should consider the position of the circulation desk and other areas in the library where a staff member will be positioned. In larger libraries with sufficient staff size, it may be advisable to place a reference desk somewhere on the library floor, so supervision is possible from more than one position.

If space permits and supervision problems will not result, consider including some seating (individual lounge chairs or benches) or small tables in the stack areas. Some shelf manufacturers offer small, carrel-like

options that are an integral part of the shelving. Consider the user: often a user wants to sit while perusing books on the shelves and doesn't want to walk a long distance to find a table. Take a good look at libraries where this is not an option and, most likely, you will find people sitting on the floor. If it isn't possible to place tables within the shelving area, at least be certain tables are located a reasonable distance from the shelves. Don't make a user walk 30 feet or more to find a place to sit down and work.

REFERENCE AREA

In most school libraries, the reference area sees heavy use. It should be spacious to allow easy access to the collection. Try to avoid using tall shelves in the reference area. Even if space is limited, you should have some shelves at lower heights.

Because many reference books are oversized, they cannot be shelved upright on standard 42-inch shelf units. A minimum of 12 inches between shelves is needed. Most manufacturers can provide units between 45 and 48 inches high at little or no additional cost, but you must request this. The tops of the shelf units can be used as work surfaces (sloped reading tops as shown in figure 6-3 are especially effective) so students can use materials while standing. Include tables and seating in the reference area, so users do not have to drag heavy reference materials to other parts of the library.

Figure 6-3
Sloped-Top Reference Shelves

ENTRANCE

Paying no attention to or placing little, if any, emphasis on planning the library entrance is a mistake to be avoided. The entrance is one of the most often overlooked features of a school library, and yet it is one of the most important; it is what your users see first. You want the entrance to make a strong, positive, and inviting statement. Another consideration when planning the entrance is the security system, if your library plans to install one. Due to ADA requirements, the detection system panels must be a minimum of 4 feet from the door. Without expert planning, this can mean a lot of wasted space at the entry. The panels must also be positioned so they are visible by and easily accessible to library staff. Finally, consider possible congestion at the entry when classes enter and exit simultaneously: the entry should be spacious enough that traffic jams will not occur. Raise these issues with the architect early in the planning process.

CIRCULATION/SERVICE AREA

Because circulation is one of the library's most heavily used areas, allow ample space around the circulation desk unobstructed by other furniture. If you can't afford empty space anywhere else in the library, this is the place it is needed most. There should be at least 6 feet of clear space in front of the circulation desk; more is preferable. When planning the circulation area, don't forget that book carts are likely to be needed here on a regular basis. Allow room to house them. You may also want to plan for a copy machine and one or more online public access catalog (OPAC) stations near the circulation desk. And you will want to include some shelving behind the circulation desk for reserve materials and frequently used reference books.

Depending on the size of the library and the number of staff, you may want to plan for a satellite service desk for a librarian somewhere on the library floor separate from the circulation desk. When properly positioned, this desk can help to increase overall visual control of the library. It also sends the positive message to users that the librarian is available and accessible.

DISPLAY

School librarians have long been aware of the importance of displays and are often frustrated by a lack of display space. Often this lack is a result of not having thought about displays when the library was designed.

Planning a new library offers an opportunity to actually design and create suitable, strategically placed display spaces. Although technology and the role the library plays as an instructional resource are both important, do not let them consume space at the expense of another equally important role: instilling the love of reading. Display is a major tool of reading promotion. A well-designed area with bulletin boards and special display furnishings can be one of the most exciting spots in a school library. Display spaces and fixtures must not be an afterthought.

For some time, the professional literature has examined bookstore marketing and design and speculated whether libraries might benefit from some of these techniques. Although the function of a school library is vastly different from that of a bookstore, school libraries are also in the business of marketing books. We do want to promote books and reading, to market our collections, and to encourage our "customers" to return again and again. Bookstore interiors can provide ideas worth incorporating into school library facility design. Look especially at face-out shelving (for display of front covers), special display furnishings, and availability of comfortable seating. Display areas in the library should be highly interesting and exciting, a showcase of materials to which people are drawn.

Research on customer behavior indicates that people entering a store tend to drift to the right. This may well apply to people entering a library, and so, if at all possible, plan for some display space to the right of the library entrance. Displays are also more likely to be noticed if they are placed in high-traffic areas of the library.

INSTRUCTIONAL AREAS

Today's school libraries are teaching spaces; instruction is an essential element of the twenty-first-century school library program, and appropriate spaces are needed for small- as well as large-group instruction. Unfortunately, many planners do not fully understand the role of the school library program and thus view instructional space as a frill rather than a necessity. As a result, many school libraries are designed without library instructional space. Ideally, a school library should have at least one classroom, conveniently located near library resources yet separate from the main library space to prevent noise from disturbing other users. In turn, instruction will be more effective when it can be done in an environment free of outside distractions.

When a separate library classroom is not available, space must be allocated on the library floor, and you will need to use furniture to define the instructional area. Try to separate the area for instruction from high-traffic areas of the library (see figure 6-4). Some libraries will require two or even three such areas, depending on the size of the school and the nature of the library program. Don't forget to make room for any instructional materials required in the area—whiteboards, projection screens, LCD projectors, monitors, and so on—and plan for some storage of teaching materials.

STUDY AREAS

Some students prefer to study alone in relatively private settings; others prefer to sit with a friend or in a group. Your furniture plan should provide for both of these user preferences; tables should be arranged to accommodate the study needs of both individuals and small groups. Often individual study spaces are not planned for, and a library is furnished with only large tables. The assump-

Figure 6-4
Study and Instruction Area in a High School Library

tion is that an individual seeking study space can share a table with others, but this does not reflect the preferences of most students. Most people looking for an individual study space prefer to sit at an empty table; once someone has claimed a space at a table, other people will try to avoid infringing on it. This is a good reason to limit the number of large tables. Students may also avoid round tables, because it is more difficult to define their own work space at a round rather than a square or rectangular table. Carrels offer secluded space for concentrated study, but not all students like them, and they can present supervision problems. If you use carrels, it is best to limit their number. Small tables, 30 or 36 inches square, are well suited for individual study space, and, because they can be combined to make larger table surfaces when needed, they are more flexible than carrels. Allow at least 5 feet between tables, which is the minimum distance from others that people need to work effectively.

Be aware that architectural plans often show chairs neatly stowed under the tables. The only time this is likely to reflect reality is when the library has been thoroughly cleaned and straightened. A plan that shows the chairs pulled out from under the tables provides a much truer sense of how the space will look and work, how crowded or uncrowded it will be. Avoid placing seat backs along heavily used traffic lanes. Most people feel vulnerable sitting with their backs to a major path of traffic and will avoid such seating.

SMALL-GROUP STUDY/PRODUCTION AREAS

The number of small-group study areas in your plan will depend on your program requirements, but you should plan for spaces of this type even if you don't envision an immediate need; small-group study areas, where groups of two to eight students can meet and work without distractions and without disturbing others, will become more and more important in the future. At least one of these spaces should be large enough to provide for some multimedia equipment and production. Versatile, easily moved furniture is a must for these areas, so the layout can be easily reconfigured.

Movable wall systems (sometimes called office partitions), available from a number of contract furniture manufacturers, are an effective way to enclose small-group spaces and isolate them from the main areas of the library. When planning the location of these systems, consider sightlines and the use of panels with glass to allow for proper visual control. Figure 6-5 illustrates this concept in a renovated high school library.

Figure 6-5

Use of Movable Wall Systems to Create a Small-Group Study Room

TECHNOLOGY

Computers are best interspersed throughout the library, but the expense of providing data and electricity connections usually limits the placement of computer workstations. Few schools can afford the luxury of a library so flexibly equipped with data drops that computers can be virtually anywhere. Even with wireless connectivity, electrical connections will still be needed. You will probably have to place computers in selected key areas of the library.

Some computers should be located at the library entrance. These may be dedicated PAC workstations. You will also want the reference area to be technology-rich to enable access to digital reference materials. Often a good configuration is to put technology areas adjacent to both the reference area and instructional areas.

Consider supervision carefully when you plan the placement of computer workstations. Try to place them where monitors can be viewed with relative ease by library staff.

PERIODICALS

The periodical section is another area that may be heavily used, and it should be spacious enough to give a relaxed and open look. Plan for some lounge seating either with or adjacent to the periodical collection.

LOUNGE SEATING

Some administrators and school librarians scoff at the idea of having lounge chairs in the library, believing this type of seating encourages socializing. If this is a concern, space the chairs well apart, or place them back to back. But do consider the student or staff member who wants to find a comfortable place to relax and get lost in the joys of reading. Furnish lounge seating areas with individual chairs; sofas or loveseats may look attractive, but avoid them unless you want to encourage conversation or other unsuitable activities. Beam or gang seating of the type used in airports and other public waiting areas is not appropriate in libraries. People do not want that kind of forced intimacy in a library. Figures 6-6 and 6-7 illustrate lounge seating in a high school and middle school library.

STORAGE OF STUDENT PROJECTS

Trends in assessment have brought about an emphasis on portfolio development to demonstrate academic growth. Providing spaces for the construction and storage of student portfolios and student-created multimedia projects should not be overlooked in the planning process. School libraries, as central depositories of information, can provide storage for these student activities. Because librarians are the information storage and retrieval experts within the school system, it is incumbent on us to raise this issue in the planning process—we may be the only ones to think about it.

Figure 6-6

Lounge Seating Area in a High School Library

Photo courtesy of Susan Weintraub, The Park School

Figure 6-7

Lounge Seating in a Middle School Library

STAFF WORK AND OFFICE AREAS

Space and furniture for staff will vary from library to library, depending on function. All school libraries require storage space and places where materials can be processed and repaired. Countertops are useful as are desk-high work surfaces. A sink is a necessity: consider the many cleaning tasks required in a school library as well as the many social functions that require easy access to a sink. Lockable space should be provided for coats and other personal effects.

Unfortunately, some school library designs have overlooked the needs of the adults who work there. School libraries need spaces for staff to work, to meet with colleagues and vendors, to plan lessons, and to have conferences with students. Ideally, storage space for staff use should be removed from the main library. However, if you have no separate office or work space, design the circulation area to include at least a minimal amount of work and storage space.

ACCESSORIES

Frequently, miscellaneous furniture items (book trucks, for example) are forgotten when the furniture plan is prepared. Take a good look at the library in which you presently work. Unless your library is highly unusual, a fair amount of "stuff" will be lying around, especially boxes. Try to include places for this "stuff" in your floor plan. Other items to consider are file cabinets (leave at least 2 feet in front of file cabinets so the drawers can be fully opened), other kinds of storage cabinets (microform, and so forth), and paperback display towers.

Considerations for Elementary School Libraries

Although libraries in elementary schools will need areas that middle and high school libraries need, there are some unique considerations. Younger children like lots of nooks and crannies (figure 6-8); therefore, it is best to avoid layouts that are overly formal or symmetrical. Aim for a more whimsical look, and incorporate spaces that are somewhat private yet easily supervised. Many students, especially the younger ones, want and need their own space.

PRIMARY AREA

In an elementary school library that serves K–6 or K–8, try to plan a primary area for younger children separate from the spaces that will be used by older students. The goal should be to provide the youngest children a piece of the library they can call their own.

STORYTELLING AREA

Architects often want to make a bold and dramatic statement with the storytelling area. Although there is nothing inherently wrong with a dramatic-looking storytelling area, it has its downsides. The storytelling area will not be in use at all times; when overall space is limited, it is best to avoid an area that will just eat up space when it is not being used. Try to provide a space that is functional, aesthetically pleasing, and flexible (with movable or stackable stools or cushions) so that the space can be used for other activities. Built-in tiered seating is often used for the storytelling area. This can

Photo courtesy of Susan Weintraub, The Park School

Figure 6-8

Reading Nook in an Elementary School Library

be effective, but it is not the most flexible solution, so again, you need to consider your overall space. If you do opt for a storytelling area with tiered seating, keep its shape intimate so no child will be far away from the storyteller. A number of examples of creative solutions for storytelling areas, and for other features of elementary school libraries, can be found in libraries that have been renovated in New York City as part of the Robin Hood Foundation's Library Initiative launched in 2002. (See Selected Readings for sources of further information about this initiative.)

Once the furniture plan is completed, study it over several days as you did the zone plan. Take yourself through the layout as if it were a typical day (if there is such a thing!), and imagine yourself as a user of the library. (Your architect may be able to show you a computer rendering with a virtual walk-through.) Changes can easily be made on paper; changes once the job is completed may be impossible.

A High School Library Furniture Plan

Figure 6-9 shows a furniture plan for a high school library (grades 9–12) developed from the bubble diagram (figure 5-2) and zone plan (figure 6-1). The school has a student population of 1,500, and the library has a print collection of 20,000 volumes and a staff of four. This library has two instructional spaces in separate rooms: a library classroom/computer lab and a videoconference/distance learning room. Although the distance learning room is for schoolwide use, it can be used for library instruction. At the top of the plan in the main part of the library, tables and seating are provided to accommodate

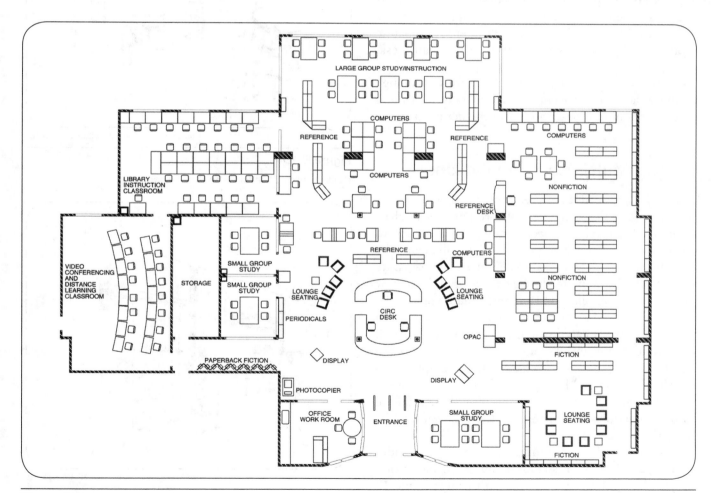

Figure 6-9

Furniture Plan for a High School Library

another class; the area is sufficiently isolated from the rest of the library so that disruption to students working elsewhere will be kept to a minimum. This area can also be used for small-group meetings during after-school or evening hours. The library also has three group-study rooms: two that accommodate four to six students and one that accommodates eight to twelve students. Visual supervision of these rooms is easily managed from the circulation desk. The library's entry vestibule works well with the theft-detection panels; they do not need to protrude into the main library space, and, in the event of an alarm, there is room between the panels and the entry doors to stop a patron. The area around the circulation/service desk is uncluttered, allowing for displays as well as obstacle-free traffic flow to all areas of the library. Because the staff office and work space is small for a library of this size, the circulation desk is large enough to provide ample work space for at least three staff members. This also encourages staff to be visible and readily available to assist students. A separate librarian desk is positioned away from the main desk, making it possible for all areas of the library to be controlled visually by library staff. There are two lounge seating areas: one adjacent to current periodicals and the circulation desk, and another in the fiction area.

Serving Multigrade Populations

Libraries that need to serve multigrade populations (K–12, K–9, middle/high school) present special challenges, and careful advance planning is necessary to answer some questions: Which materials will need to be separate and which will need to be shared? Are separate areas for the different age levels needed, and, if so, how can this be accomplished? Reference materials are the most easily shared resources; if the reference area has a central location, it can divide the overall space and still be easily accessible by all grade levels. Usually there is a need to divide the fiction collection (for example, middle school fiction and high school fiction); when this is done, it is good to provide seating near these separate fiction collections designated for the grade levels for which the books are intended.

For a renovated facility at the Park School, an independent, coeducational school in suburban Baltimore, Maryland, for 885 pre-kindergarten through grade 12 students, designers found a creative way to separate the lower-school and upper-school sections of the com-

bined library facility. A common wall provides reading nooks and book display space on the side facing the lower-school section of the library, and the side of the wall facing the upper-school section provides individual study carrels. Figures 6-10 and 6-11 show the architect's rendering of the plan for this wall.

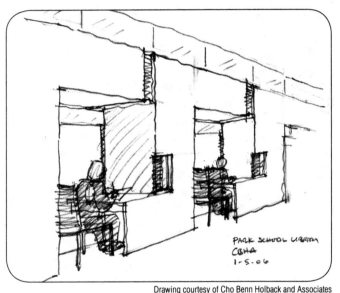

Drawing courtesy of Cho Benn Holback and Associates

Figure 6-10

Built-in Study Carrels, The Park School

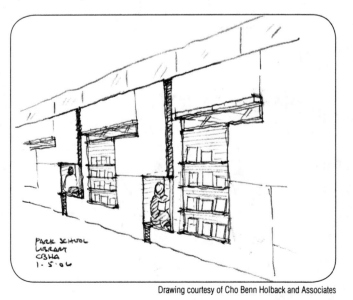

Drawing courtesy of Cho Benn Holback and Associates

Figure 6-11

Built-in Reading Cubbies, The Park School

The design of a combined library facility for a new K–12 island school fifteen miles off the coast of Maine presented the challenge of how best to provide materials and spaces for four distinct learning groups, all in one shared facility. Added to that challenge was the fact that the school is small: it serves only 210 students. The financial constraints for building a school for that small a population inevitably require that every square foot of the library be meticulously planned, and some difficult compromises have to be made. The planning documents called for two entrances to the library, one for grades K–5 and one for grades 6–12. The furniture plan (figure 6-12) placed the circulation/service desk in the center but at the rear of the library, away from the entrances. This location makes it possible for library staff to be adjacent to both the main use and the staff areas of the library. Positioning the desk near the entrances would have been a less than ideal solution, and because there was no plan for a theft-detection system, that reason for locating the desk near the entrances was eliminated. The central core of the library is a shared use space: print reference materials and computers for access to digital resources (figure 6-13). On one side of this core are materials and seating for the middle and high school students; on the other side, materials, seating,

Figure 6-13

Library Interior, Vinalhaven School

and a storytelling area for elementary school students. The design of the school was based on creating separate "islands" for grades K–2, 3–5, middle school, and high school, along with a "discovery island."

> These islands branch off the heart of the school—the library. This concept evolved from the idea that although islands seem separated from the mainland, in reality they are connected below the water. The design separates the grades into islands by building wings, but maintains the connections through the library.[1]

The Result of Exemplary Planning

Established in 1980, Colegio Los Nogales is a bilingual (Spanish/English) K–12 school in Bogotá, Colombia. The diverse staff provides students with international role models skilled in teaching a curriculum based on a global perspective.

A member of the school's board of directors, having observed schools in the United States and other countries, began to consider how library information technology resources—particularly telecommunications—could influence teaching and learning at the school. She drafted, and the board of directors adopted, an educational philosophy that included an information/literary curriculum centered on a state-of-the-art library media program.

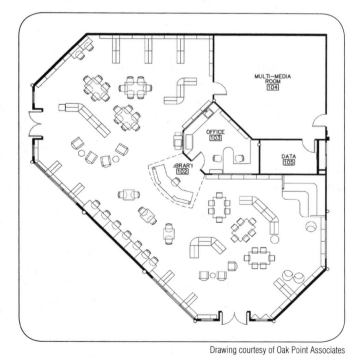

Figure 6-12

Furniture Plan, Vinalhaven School

Planning, Design, and Construction

A library media center facility was designed that would house exciting, coordinated library and information technology programs. Focus remained on the delivery of services and the instructional program, not on the glitz and glamour of a showplace.

After several interim steps, the facility design was approved. The design positioned the library inside the traffic patterns where it could be easily accessed by all levels of students, who study in four separate but adjacent buildings: preschool, primary, middle school, and upper school. It is interesting to note that the new facility was at the edge of the campus—until the school bought the property across the street and put the sports programs there. The library is now in the exact center of the campus.

Interviews with staff and faculty members, parents, and students formed the basis for the facility's design and size. The design included offices; work space and equipment closets; traditional spaces for storytelling, research, circulation, reference, and instruction; an atrium for rotating Colombiana exhibits; a second-floor outdoor reading terrace; a large teacher preparation room; individual study cabinets; and conference rooms.

Concurrently, program goals and objectives were identified, strategic plans for the library and technology programs were developed, and action plans were initiated. Professional development was an important component of these plans, along with new job descriptions and policy and procedure changes. Plans for collection development were also prepared.

The architect developed a space conception that established the general shape of the building and a size of 11,000 square feet. A zone plan, based on a bubble diagram, was developed to reflect program requirements. Traffic patterns were of utmost importance. The zone plan was modified three times before general agreement was reached. In the final plan, primary and upper-school areas were separated to a degree, but not by fixed or load-bearing walls. This feature provided flexibility for future program shifts.

Interior design issues were then addressed. Communication between the architect, the library consultant, and faculty members was constant and abundant. Figure 6-14 shows the final architectural drawing and furniture plan.

Throughout the construction phase, the program planning documents guided resource selection, the development of staffing patterns and job descriptions, policy and procedure revisions, and staff development. Staff development helped teachers to integrate technologies and information into the instructional program as well as broaden their view of the library as a full partner in the instructional process. This advance implementation of program elements made possible the immediate full use of the facility at the time of occupancy.

Design Revisited

It is now five years since the new library opened, and very few people at the school remember the time when it didn't exist. As intended, the library has indeed become the heart of the school. The collection has grown by 50 percent, and students are checking out and reading more books each year. An increasing number of teachers are collaborating with librarians to develop inquiry-based units that integrate library curricula with the content area. For both teachers and students, technology has become necessary and useful in searching for and using information.

These results would not have been possible without a meticulously planned facility with a flexible design that allows adaptation to meet the changing needs of the community and the ever-increasing demands for technology. For example, five years ago when the facility first opened, the library's collection was only partially automated, and the technical processes area was used entirely to catalog and process a large number of volumes. At the same time, demand in the preschool and primary school sections started to grow, and teachers sought to use the library on a flexible schedule. In a single, integrated space, such use was not compatible with the fixed schedule of workshops. So, in the fourth year, when most of the book processing had concluded, the technical processes area was remodeled as a library classroom for the preschool and primary school sections, while a small area was retained for technical processes.

Other areas of the library have also changed from their original use and have been adapted to new purposes. The second floor, for example, has housed an exhibition center, a mobile computer lab, and a reading room for older teens; its use will continue to evolve, depending on the demands of the community.

Even with exemplary planning, minor problems often become apparent once the facility is in use. Some of the library media center's characteristic features, such as the multiple entrances and circulation spaces, have

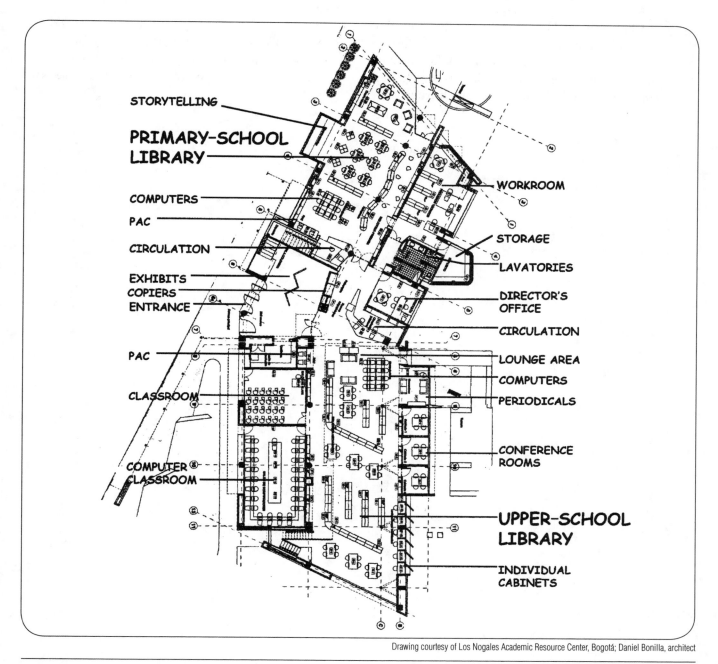

STORYTELLING

PRIMARY-SCHOOL LIBRARY

COMPUTERS

PAC

CIRCULATION

EXHIBITS
COPIERS
ENTRANCE

PAC

CLASSROOM

COMPUTER
CLASSROOM

WORKROOM

STORAGE

LAVATORIES

DIRECTOR'S
OFFICE

CIRCULATION

LOUNGE AREA

COMPUTERS

PERIODICALS

CONFERENCE
ROOMS

UPPER-SCHOOL LIBRARY

INDIVIDUAL
CABINETS

Drawing courtesy of Los Nogales Academic Resource Center, Bogotá; Daniel Bonilla, architect

Figure 6-14

Furniture Plan, Ground Floor: Colegio Los Nogales, Bogotá, Colombia

created control issues that staff have had to learn to manage—who enters and leaves, which doors should be locked and which should remain open, and how to minimize noise and interruptions caused by students and teachers using the library as a shortcut to other areas of the school. Additionally, the beautiful high ceilings of the secondary school section pose acoustical problems. The noise level tends to rise, especially when there are several groups working downstairs and several working upstairs.

Nevertheless, the results of exemplary planning are evident. The open, well-lighted, vivid atmosphere has contributed to making the library the center of the school. There are no hiding places and no hidden spaces. There are no barriers among books, working spaces, people, computers; the building is a metaphor for the openness and flexibility of lifelong learners.

NOTE

1. National School Boards Association, "Vinalhaven School, Vinalhaven, Maine," *Learning by Design 2004* (April 2004), http://www.asbj.com/lbd/2004/projects/vinalhaven.pdf.

7

Creating an Inviting Interior
Furnishings

Be imaginative. Think inviting. One of America's greatest creative geniuses, Ray Bradbury exemplifies imagination at its most creative. We want school libraries to be learning spaces that students will choose as destinations, spaces that participants in the Library Power initiative funded by the DeWitt Wallace–Reader's Digest Foundation recognized "as places of comfort and pleasure where students can pursue their own dreams and ideas."[1] A twelfth grader in a school where the library media center was refurbished through the New York Life Foundation's Revitalizing High School Libraries project expresses a similar sentiment: "Honestly, the aesthetic aspect . . . makes a big difference in the way the students view the Media Center, and so . . . improving the inside encourages pupils to enter and take part [in] the library's resources."[2] Keith Curry Lance's research, which demonstrates that students who visit their school library more frequently improve their reading and writing scores, gives us a compelling reason to create library interiors in which students will want to spend time.[3] This chapter is intended to provide you with a basic understanding of furniture and interior design issues, with information to help you be a more knowledgeable consumer. Choosing furniture wisely will do much to create a comfortable, visually stimulating school library interior, a memorable place that will inspire creativity.

Furniture Selection

As with every other phase in the library design process, library staff members need to be actively involved in the selection of furniture. Although providing proper furniture is only one of many phases in the library planning process, it is a critical phase, and its importance should not be diminished. Because the selection of furniture is so important, it is another aspect of the design process where the librarian, who may be inexperienced in designing libraries and selecting library furniture, can surely benefit from professional assistance.

In her 1990 publication *Planning School Library Media Facilities*, Pauline Anderson writes, "Time was when most of the furniture coming from traditional library furniture companies had a monotonous sameness but that day is long gone."[4] It is true that library furniture design has improved to the extent that there is no longer any reason school library interiors should be drab, dull, and boring. Yet school library interiors that do not give the impression of monotonous sameness are still the exception, rather than the rule.

Why is this? Perhaps school planners fail to budget sufficiently for furniture because they do not recognize the importance of furnishings. Perhaps they do not investigate furniture options thoroughly, and instead buy only furniture available through school or library supply catalogs. Perhaps they too readily accept the recommendations made by architect-hired furniture consultants, who can save a lot of time, money, and effort if they specify the same items of furniture over and over again, year after year, for every project. Or perhaps they judge furniture solely on its sturdiness and serviceability without considering aesthetics.

Certainly one must look for sturdy and serviceable library furniture, but these attributes can be as easily found in furniture that is pleasing to the eye as they can in furniture that is mundane. Some library planners advocate buying plain, sturdy, serviceable furniture for school libraries, arguing that contemporary design will soon go out of fashion. Of course, it is important to choose contemporary design with care and to avoid obviously faddish or trendy furniture, but good design is timeless: one has only to look at Breuer's Wassily chair or the Corbusier Bentwood chair, both of which remain stylish today even though they were designed many years ago.

Furniture selection is the one phase of the library planning process where everyone may feel expertly qualified. Most people are familiar with furniture because they select it for their homes, but selecting furniture for library use is not the same as selecting furniture for the home. For one thing, it is not possible to run to the nearest mall and visit a library furniture store.

Sources for Furniture

An amazing variety of furniture is available, much of it created for markets other than the library market, but nonetheless appropriate for library use. Here is a fact known to few librarians: there is a lot of furniture out there from nonlibrary furniture manufacturers that is perfectly suitable for library use. In fact, some of it is more suitable than what is traditionally thought of as library furniture.

Furniture for libraries comes from one of three sources: library suppliers, which sell furniture from library furniture manufacturers; contract furniture manufacturers; or suppliers of custom-made furniture designed for a specific job.

Library Suppliers

Some library furniture manufacturers—Worden, for example—operate in much the same way as a contract furniture manufacturer. Other manufacturers, such as Brodart, offer their products through library suppliers but sell additional contract furniture through various retailers. Most major library suppliers offer a number of economical furniture items and are, therefore, especially good sources when the furniture budget is minimal. Although it may make your job easier, you should resist the temptation to limit your search for furniture to these sources. This is not to say they don't offer good products, but by looking no farther than the library suppliers, you are greatly limiting your options.

Contract Furniture

Contract furniture is a large, hidden market—hidden to anyone, that is, with no interior design experience. Few librarians know anything about this market, because its products are manufactured primarily for business. But it is furniture worth knowing about. The trick is knowing how to tap this market, how to find out what is available.

Firms known as furniture rep groups represent most contract furniture manufacturers and cover different geographical territories. You can obtain contact information for a local representative group from the manufacturers you are interested in. (See appendix G for a list of furniture manufacturers.) From this group, you can obtain the names of furniture dealers and furniture sales outlets. Most furniture manufacturers have showrooms, and some furniture dealers have showrooms or working showrooms, but few of them are open to the public, and an appointment is usually required to visit them. For this reason it is beneficial if the architectural firm either employs or works with an interior designer or a library consultant familiar with contract furniture. These design professionals can greatly expand the furniture possibilities for you to consider. However, it is still possible to find out about contract furniture without the assistance of a design professional; it just takes time and persistence.

Visiting library conferences where manufacturers exhibit is another way of learning about furniture. Several furniture manufacturers exhibit at ALA conferences. At the state and regional levels, public library associations may have exhibits of furniture. And, as with everything else in the process of planning a new library facility, visiting other new libraries will help. Visit all types of libraries, identify furniture you like, and find out where this furniture was obtained.

One word of caution is in order when selecting contract furniture for a library. Because some contract furniture is manufactured specifically for the business market, some items may not be built to last as long as furniture in libraries needs to last. Furniture in business settings does not get the same amount of use and abuse as furniture in libraries, and many businesses can afford to replace furniture more often than schools can. It is important, therefore, to pay close attention to durability when evaluating contract furniture.

Custom Furniture

Although you should approach custom-built furniture with caution, do not dismiss it altogether, particularly if you have an idea for an unusual piece of furniture. Custom-built furniture may be a good option for specialty items: display furniture, risers for a storytelling area, or a circulation desk. Furniture can also be custom-constructed to complement the library's interior architecture, and for this reason architects often like to use it. Custom-built furniture may be more or less expensive than a similar article found in a catalog, depending on materials used. Exercise caution when determining the quality of the finished piece. If you are promised custom-made furniture built to the same standard as manufactured furniture, you may or may not get what was promised. Specifications for any custom-made furniture should require conformity with quality standards provided by the Architectural Woodwork Institute (AWI). You should also require that the manufacturer be an AWI member. Many times, custom-made furniture will be built in—that is, actually a part of the architecture; this precludes flexibility, and moving built-in furniture is costly, if not impossible. Furthermore, custom furniture is not performance tested, nor does it have a service history.

Criteria for Purchasing Furniture

When buying furniture, there are many technicalities concerning construction, materials, and testing to consider—literally more than any one librarian would ever have time to learn. But there are certain things you must know in order to make any informed decisions, or to make sure that whoever is making decisions for you makes them correctly.

The following criteria must be considered when purchasing furniture for a school library.

Appearance

Although appearance should not be the most important criterion, it is listed first because too often it is given no consideration. Handsome furniture will help to create an exciting, comfortable, joyous atmosphere; furniture with plain, uninspired design will not. Furniture for school libraries should also be age appropriate. Our students are children and teenagers, and they are more comfortable with furniture that is youthful in appearance. Furniture should also enhance the architecture and work favorably to create the desired atmosphere and environment. If you have high-quality, relatively new existing furniture that can be reused or cost-effectively refurbished for use in a new facility, be certain that it will be compatible with the architecture and with any new furniture that will be purchased.

Functionality

The furniture for a library must fit its intended use. Review the activities that will take place in the library, and make sure that the furniture will accommodate them. Pay particular attention to wire-management features of furniture where electrical and data connections will be needed.

Comfort

The comfort of the furniture must not be ignored—we want our students to be comfortable as they work. Why is this important? "Studies have shown that furniture that is not designed for the user, or sized to fit, will result in listlessness, time off-task and loss of valuable educational time."[5] One school superintendent, when new student chairs were to be purchased for the school library, insisted they not be too comfortable, because students should not be encouraged to hang around the library too long. Think about it! Ergonomics (discussed in chapter 8) involves issues of both comfort and health, and ergonomic features need to be considered as part of the comfort criterion.

Durability and Ease of Maintenance

School library furniture probably takes more abuse than furniture in any other library setting, and it must hold up to heavy use for a long time with minimal maintenance. Manufactured furniture should be tested for durability and the test results made available to you. Probably the best means of checking on the durability of an item is to speak with someone who has had experience with it. Manufacturers should supply you with references you can contact as well as warranty information. Avoid furniture with lots of texture—it will be harder to clean, and idle fingers will likely try to embellish it. Furniture should be easy to clean and easy to repair. Any upholstered furniture should be easy to reupholster. Involve maintenance staff with evaluating durability and ease of maintenance; they know what to look for.

Safety

Avoid furniture with sharp edges, paying particular attention to table edges (see figure 7-1). Chairs and tables need to be well balanced and heavy enough so they do not tip easily. Wall shelving should be properly attached to the wall. Double-faced shelving units over 42 inches high must not stand alone but should be combined with other units.

Sustainability

The criterion of sustainability—resource use that does not adversely affect the environment—is becoming more and more important in schools. Its application to library furnishings is discussed in chapter 9.

Flammability

Furniture and fabrics in public buildings must meet flammability standards, which vary from state to state and city to city. There are two main flammability codes—California Technical Bulletin 117 (TB 117) and California Technical Bulletin 133 (TB 133). TB 133 is the more stringent—it is a full-scale fire test for a com-

Figure 7-1
Avoid Sharp Edges

plete piece of furniture—and is becoming an industry standard for fire safety in public buildings.

Price

Up to a point, it is true that you will get what you pay for. If you buy a task chair for $89, for example, you simply will not get the quality you would get if you paid $600. On the other hand, quality cannot always be measured by price. An item of furniture from a well-known designer may be priced higher simply because of the designer's reputation. The piece may indeed be of good quality, but if, for example, it is twice the price of a similar item, it may not be of twice the quality.

Key Features

For each type of furniture, you need to be aware of particular features.

Shelving

Because shelving is a major part of any furniture budget, and because it usually needs to last the lifetime of the building, it must be chosen with care. This is not an item on which it is wise to scrimp. If the furniture budget is minimal, give shelving top priority. Because of the weight of books, library shelves need to be extremely strong—strong enough to bear prescribed loads (approximately 100 pounds per shelf) without sagging, bending, leaning, swaying, or collapsing. Because library shelving has very specific requirements, it is best to buy it from a reputable library furniture manufacturer, one that builds shelving specifically for the library market.

Library shelving comes in two basic types of construction: cantilever (or bracket) and case-style. Cantilever-style shelving consists of two upright support columns to which shelves are attached by brackets. The columns are supported by a base and a top crossbar. Case-style shelving consists of upright panels from which shelves are supported by pins that are fitted into holes in the upright panels. (Tamper-proof pins are essential: when a shelf is in place, it should not be possible to remove the pins.) The upright panels are supported either by a base and top or by an interior steel frame. Either type of shelving is suitable for library use. Cantilever shelving is the most commonly used type of shelving, and it is often the most economical solution.

Shelving can be all wood, all steel, or a combination of wood and steel. All-wood shelving is generally too expensive for most school libraries. Good-quality steel shelving, especially welded frame construction, will serve your needs well for less money. Keep in mind that books and materials cover up much of the surface of shelving, so the steel parts will not be all that visible. And what is visible can be in a color chosen to enhance the overall look of the library. (Be aware that darker colors show dust and scratches more readily.)

Adding wood- or laminate-covered end panels and canopy tops to cantilever-style steel shelving will do much to dress it up (see figure 7-2 for a variety of end panel designs). Graphics can be printed from digital images on materials such as acrylic, vinyl, metal, and tempered glass to create one-of-a-kind end panels. Students could create the artwork for the panels, which would introduce an unusual design element into the library as well as involve the kids in the building project (see figure 7-3). Some shelving is available with

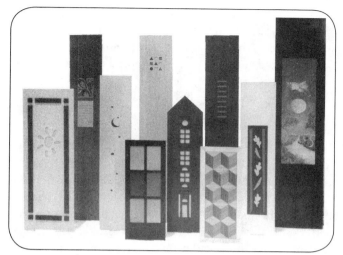

Photo © TMC Furniture, Inc.

Figure 7-2

End Panels (TMC Furniture, Inc.)

Photo courtesy of TotaLibra

Figure 7-3

End Panel (TotaLibra)

an open base, which can give the library an airy, more spacious look (see figure 7-4). If you choose open-base shelving, keep in mind that cleaning underneath will be required (and students may be tempted to use these hidden spaces as trash receptacles).

Compact movable shelving has generally not been used in school libraries, because it is more expensive than conventional shelving, and because it increases floor-loading requirements, which adds to the cost of construction. Also, it limits the ability to browse, so it is most appropriate for materials that need limited access (textbooks, for example). Compact movable shelving is an option to consider for storage, for materials in process in staff areas, or for seldom-used special collections. Also, it is worth considering for other shelving needs in high school libraries when space is minimal. If you do decide to include any compact movable shelving, be certain what you purchase has adequate safety features and is easy to operate.

Here are some specific features to look for in shelving:

Adjustable-height shelves that are easy to adjust without tools or excessive effort. Holes for shelf pins should be at increments of no more than 1 inch.

Photo courtesy of TotaLibra

Figure 7-4

Metis Shelving System (TotaLibra)

Integral backs 1 to 2 inches high to prevent books from falling off the back of shelves or sliding through.

Ease of leveling.

Ease of assembly and disassembly—sometimes shelving must be moved.

Durable finish that can endure normal use and cleaning for at least thirty years without sign of wear.

Most shelving units are available with built-in book supports. Supports that operate from a trough at the back of the shelf are more effective than supports that are fastened to the underside of the shelf above (these supports tend to bend, and books can easily slide under the supports). Before specifying any type of built-in book support, try it out; test it for ease of operation and durability. Some librarians prefer separate book supports to built-ins, and an 8- or 9-inch-high heavy-duty steel support, with a cork or other type of nonskid base, may well be the most practical and cost-effective option.

For libraries located in seismic zones, shelving must be designed and installed to meet codes for that area. (Any shelving installation must comply with all applicable federal, state, and local codes.)

Shelving comes in standard 36-inch widths (some manufacturers offer 20- and 24-inch widths as well), and in either single- or double-faced configurations. A variety of heights is available, and there are slight differences in heights from one manufacturer to the next. For general information on shelving and shelf capacities, refer to appendix D. Because school libraries never seem to be big enough, one is often obliged to use 72-inch or higher shelving. Keep in mind the comfort level, however, and try to keep shelving low and accessible. No one enjoys having to stretch and bend, and using stools is hazardous. It is best to limit the height of shelving to 72 inches for high school libraries. Depending on applicable building codes, freestanding shelving 60 inches or higher may require floor anchoring for stability; higher shelving may also require horizontal bracing. If you must use tall shelving, try to include some units at 42 to 48 inches, even in high schools; covered with laminate tops, these units can then be used as stand-up work surfaces (see figure 7-5). Shelves 45 to 48 inches tall with sloped tops are especially desirable in the reference area (see chapter 6 for further information).

Users and staff members alike often complain about the difficulty of reading the titles and spine labels of

Photo courtesy of John J. Adams, School Furnishings, Inc.

Figure 7-5

Custom Canopy Top (Bretford Manufacturing, Inc.)

From *The Librarian from the Black Lagoon,* copyright © 1997
by Mike Thaler and Jared Lee. Reprinted by permission of Scholastic, Inc.

Figure 7-6

"If you twist your neck and squint, you can read the spines."

books stored on bottom shelves. The children's book *The Librarian from the Black Lagoon* illustrates this situation with tongue in cheek (see figure 7-6), but the problem is all too real. Solutions exist—just look at the shelving in bookstores. The bottom shelf, or even the bottom two or three shelves, can be sloped. This type of shelving does require more floor space: single-shelf units are from 5 to 6 inches deeper than conventional, nonsloping shelf units. Consider using some shelving of this type, especially to house those parts of the collection that are heavily used or to display new items.

Shelving is also available with heavy-duty casters for easy mobility. This type of shelving is appropriate for areas of the library where you may need to move shelving occasionally to make space for some activity. Options include casters that can be locked to hold the shelving in place, and units with either concealed or exposed casters. Casters should not be used on units higher than 64 inches.

Finally, you need to consider shelving for paperback collections, unless you plan to shelve all paperbacks with hardcover books. You can purchase regular shelving in a depth suitable for paperbacks (8 to 10 inches), freestanding paperback display spinners, wall-mounted display spinners, or paperback displayers that attach to the ends of shelving units. Media collections will also need specialty shelving or display furniture.

Work Surfaces

Tables in a school library are needed for two basic functions: (1) studying and reading, and (2) using computers. The purpose of a table will determine its size and features.

STUDY TABLES

Study or reading tables come in a number of sizes, shapes, and styles. (Figure 7-7 shows an example of a study table.) Your architect might encourage the use of large, rectangular tables. Architects tend to like large tables, arguing that they complement big spaces. Small tables are more flexible; they can be moved more readily and can easily be combined to create a larger working space. Keep in mind, however, that smaller tables tip more easily than larger tables. Consequently, when specifying small tables, the weight of the table is particularly important. Tables come in various heights, and the height chosen should be appropriate for the age of the intended user. Appendix E lists age-appropriate table heights. Consider adding some adjustable-height tables for use by students in wheelchairs. (Chapter 10 discusses ADA guidelines and requirements for work surface heights.)

Photo and product courtesy of The Worden Company

Figure 7-7
Alcott Table (The Worden Company)

COMPUTER TABLES

Computer tables need to be equipped for wire management and must be large enough to accommodate computer hardware, with room left over for a usable work surface. If you take a good look around libraries, you will notice that computer workstations are often cramped and uncomfortable to use. Tables for computers must be at least 24 inches deep for LCD monitors and 30 inches deep for CRT monitors. Width should be a minimum of 36 inches; 42 to 48 inches is much better. Thirty inches, a width commonly specified by architects and designers, is not sufficient. Keep in mind 30 inches are required just for the keyboard and mouse pad; to be comfortable for the user, an additional 14 inches should be available for a notebook or tablet, with some additional room left over for books and other items. Sixty inches is an ideal width, especially when two students must work at one computer. And keep in mind that younger students work best in small groups, so you may want to plan work surface widths that will accommodate three or four students working together. If you specify tables with CPU storage under the work surface, be certain CPUs are not placed where they can easily be kicked or bumped by feet, knees, or chairs.

TABLE CONSTRUCTION

The construction of tables is extremely important, because construction techniques will determine the stability of the table. The simplest type of table construction is a plain tabletop supported by four legs. To add stability, tables are often made with either stretchers

(crosspieces that connect the legs together) or aprons (pieces of wood that run just under the top, connecting the legs), or a combination of both. Technically, the addition of stretchers or aprons adds strength to the table. However, stretchers can be a problem in libraries, because students will use them as footrests, adding to the wear and tear on the table. Aprons can also be a problem, because they reduce the clearance space under the tabletop. Tables without stretchers are more accessible to users in wheelchairs, are easier to clean around, and offer more flexibility in chair placement. If you choose a simple four-legged table, construction of the leg-to-tabletop joint is of utmost importance, because only the legs support the tabletop. Get the best quality joint construction your budget will allow. The strongest joint is metal-to-metal: bolts or screws that go into a metal fastener placed in the top or leg join the top and leg. Tables with panel ends are worth considering if you want to restrict the placement of chairs at the table ends. This can be important when tables are placed at the edge of a traffic lane.

Another type of table to consider is a sloped-top reading table. These are often found in elementary libraries, and, interestingly, they tend to be very popular in middle and high school libraries, perhaps because a sloped top is quite comfortable to use. It is also easier for students with visual impairments to read at a table with a sloped top. A table of this style can be very effective and useful in the reference area. Be certain the bottom edge of the table has a book stop to prevent books and other items from sliding off. If you choose this style table for a middle or high school library, specify one without a center book display trough.

TABLETOPS

Tabletops are available in either wood or particleboard. Quality wood is strong but expensive. Particleboard is an acceptable alternative, but keep in mind that the strength of particleboard is determined by its thickness. Finishes for particleboard tops include veneer, high-pressure laminate (HPL), thermofused melamine (TFM; also referred to as low-pressure laminate), and linoleum. Veneers are often as thin as paper and do not wear well. Laminate and linoleum tops are quite durable and reasonably easy to clean, and they are a good means of bringing color into the library, but be careful with color selection. Solid colors show more dirt and scratches than do patterned colors. Select a neutral color that is neither too light nor too dark; very light colors can cause glare, and dark colors contribute to eyestrain. Linoleum is a natural, biodegradable product. With the increasing emphasis on sustainability, linoleum is worth considering. Also, unlike laminate, linoleum keeps its color all the way through, and surface cuts and scratches will actually grow back together after a period of time. There are also oils available that can recondition and repair linoleum. Tabletops with round or bullnose edges are safer than sharper edged alternatives. Avoid self-edged laminates, as they will not hold up to heavy use.

Seating

More than any other item of library furniture, chairs present a bewildering number of choices. Choose carefully, because chairs will be heavily used and abused, so strength and durability are of the utmost concern. Consider also that the sheer number of chairs will have a strong impact on the overall look of the library interior. If you want to bring some style and pizzazz into your library, abandon the notion that you absolutely must buy that traditional square seat, squared-back, so-called library chair that has been lingering in the library furniture market for the past four decades.

People use libraries, including school libraries, for many different purposes. It makes sense to serve these different purposes by providing different types of seating, rather than relying on just one type of chair for use throughout the library. The following different types of chairs should be considered.

READING/STUDY CHAIRS

You will probably order more reading/study chairs than any other type. You can choose from a number of different styles, from the classic to the contemporary. Figures 7-8 through 7-10 show three different styles for this type of chair. (Figure 7-10, an option to an all-wood chair, is a "sustainable" chair made from wood and woven recycled postindustrial automotive seat belting.) Chairs should complement the study tables in both style and color and should complement the architecture as well.

The seat height of the chair will depend on the age for which it is intended. Appendix E lists age-appropriate chair heights. You will need to decide if you want chairs with or without arms. Chairs with arms offer additional comfort, but students often find it tempting to sit on the arms. If you do get chairs with arms, be absolutely certain they will fit under the tables without damaging either the chair arm or the tabletop. Upholstered arms will not wear well, so it is best to avoid them.

Photo and product courtesy of The Worden Company

Figure 7-8
Turner Chair (The Worden Company)

Xylon® Chair designed by Giancarlo Piretti and manufactured in the U.S.A. by Krueger International, Inc., under license from Pro-Cord s.r.l.

Figure 7-9
Piretti Xylon Chair (Krueger International, Inc.)

Photo courtesy of Peter Danko Designs

Figure 7-10
Arborline Side Chair (The Danko Design Initiative)

Upholstered seats, or seats and backs, add comfort and can be considered, as long as the upholstery is of good quality and can easily be replaced.

Some librarians prefer sled-base chairs. The sled base adds stability and distributes weight more evenly. Some of the available sled bases can accommodate two or three seated positions, allowing the user to lean either forward or back; these chairs are popular with students (see figures 7-11 and 7-12). One disadvantage is that sled bases become scuffed and marred.

Photo courtesy of Sauder Manufacturing Co.

Figure 7-11

Mission Three-Position Chair (Sauder Contract)

LOUNGE CHAIRS

Lounge chairs are often upholstered, but like other library chairs, arms should not be upholstered. The fabric should be easy to maintain; slipcover upholstery is best. There should be a space between the back and seat to prevent dirt and objects from collecting in a crevice (see figure 7-13). With this latter criterion, you will find the options for lounge chairs drastically reduced. An option to an upholstered lounge chair is shown in figure 7-14, a lounge chair similar in construction and materials to the study chair shown in figure 7-10. Students may have a tendency to move lounge chairs. If you want to avoid this, consider the weight of the chair you select. The heavier the chair, the less likely it will be moved. High school libraries should consider purchasing some lounge chairs with tablet arms for laptop computer use (see figure 7-15).

TASK CHAIRS

Task chairs should be considered for computer workstations. They are more comfortable than reading chairs for computer work, and the user can make adjustments as needed. Figure 7-16 shows a task chair suitable for school libraries. When selecting chairs with casters, keep in mind students may tend to use the wheels more often than you'd like; task chairs with height-adjustment features can be purchased without

Ithaca Side Chair photo courtesy of Bretford

Figure 7-12

Ithaca Two-Position Chair (Bretford Manufacturing, Inc.)

Available from Group Four Furniture, Inc., Toronto, Ontario.
Archer design by David Wheeler.

Figure 7-13

Archer Lounge Chair (Group Four Furniture, Inc.)

casters. It is not necessary to get a chair with many different kinds of adjustments. These may encourage play, and they have more mechanisms that can go wrong. Pneumatic height is the one adjustment feature you'll want, however, with the minimum range between 16 and 20.5 inches. The seat depth of a task chair should be between 15 and 17 inches, and the seat width 18.2 inches minimum. Seats should have a waterfall front (contour built into the seat front). Task chairs are available with or without arms, in hard-shell polypropylene, or with upholstered seats or upholstered seats and backs. Task chairs and stools for staff use should have more adjustability, with upholstered seat and back, and casters.

CLASSROOM CHAIRS

For an instructional area, consider using a sturdy, stackable chair. Stackable chairs are no longer what they were—mundane and used primarily for large meeting spaces. The ability to stack can be useful, and purchasing this type of chair for some of the library seating may allow you to buy a more expensive reading/study chair. Stackable chairs most often have metal legs. Be certain they will be durable enough for library use.

MISCELLANEOUS SEATING

Benches and built-in window seats are another type of seating to consider, particularly in the fiction area. Use single-seat benches. If you have stand-up computer stations, you may want to provide high stools. Be certain they are well balanced and will not tip over easily.

FABRICS

Fabrics that wear well include wool, wool/nylon blends, olefin, and trevira. Patterns and tweeds in medium to dark colors will show less dirt and wear than solid, light colors.

Photo courtesy of Peter Danko Designs

Figure 7-14

Gotham Lounge Chair (The Danko Design Initiative)

Photo and product courtesy of The Worden Company

Figure 7-15

American Classics Lounge Chair (The Worden Company)

Photo courtesy of Virco

Figure 7-16

Zuma Task Chair (Virco)

For all types of seating, specify glides or casters appropriate for the planned floor covering, so chairs can be moved easily and without damage to the floor. If any chairs are to be placed against a wall, provide some type of protection on the wall surface.

Circulation Desk

The circulation desk is often the first piece of furniture a student sees when entering a library, and its design should convey a welcoming message. The desk should have a distinctive look to announce itself as a library service point and should be planned carefully, because staff members spend a great deal of time there. If it is not functional or does not meet your specific needs, the desk will be a constant and permanent irritation. More than any other furniture item, the circulation desk requires the librarian to be involved in planning features and details. Do not leave it entirely in the hands of the architect. Examples of the most successful circulation desks are those that have been planned to the last detail by the librarian.

Circulation desks are available in manufactured, modular components, or they can be custom built. Depending on materials used, a custom-built desk can be more affordable. As with any custom-built furniture, however, caution is advised. A custom-built circulation desk will generally be one piece, and there will be little, if any, possibility of moving it. If needs change and the circulation desk requires modification, this will be more difficult if not impossible with a custom-built desk. Another consideration is wire management: a custom-made desk may not have the same quality wire-management features as one purchased from a furniture manufacturer, so you will need to clearly specify your needs. If you choose to have a circulation desk custom made, be certain to specify what goes under the counters: drawers, storage space, knee space, and so on. Once the design for a custom-built desk is done, the designer will provide shop drawings that must be approved before construction begins. Be certain you are given the chance to review the shop drawings, and scrutinize them carefully.

Modular components from office furniture manufacturers are another choice for the circulation desk. This option can work especially well when both office and work spaces need to be incorporated into the circulation area.

Begin the design of your circulation desk by listing all the functions that will take place at the desk along with all the features you want, including the number of computer workstations required, the number of staff members who will work at the desk at any one time, and whether or not the desk must include a book return unit (with space underneath for a depressible book truck). This will determine the length of the desk you need. Library furniture catalogs are a good source of ideas for the various features available. Be certain to plan for storage space, and leave room for knee space under the desk for those places where staff members will work. Unbelievable as it may seem, it is not uncommon to find circulation desks where every inch is devoted to storage, with no room for anyone to sit! Be certain there will be sufficient electrical, data, and telephone connections at the desk—in most cases outlets for these connections will need to be under the desk on the floor—and good wire-management features. Also, be certain the front of the desk has some type of kick base. If you have some specialized needs that cannot be met by using stock items, most manufacturers are able to make custom modifications.

To function well, circulation desks should have different work surface heights to fit different tasks. For seated work, or in elementary school libraries, the surface height should be 29 inches. Standard adult standing height is 39 inches. To accommodate a computer workstation, a minimum depth of 30 inches is preferred. To prevent equipment from protruding beyond the work surface, you may want to consider more depth for those parts of the desk where computers or any other large equipment will be placed. The parts of the desk where patron transactions will take place should be no more than 30 inches deep; otherwise, reaching across the work surface will be difficult. Also, to comply with ADA regulations, the circulation desk should have one section at least 36 inches wide and no more than 36 inches high, and this section must be located on an accessible route. If written transactions are required at the desk, you must design the section with knee space a minimum of 19 inches deep to allow a user in a wheelchair to pull under the desktop.

Once you have the design of the circulation desk laid out, it is worth taking the time to make a two-dimensional model. Cut out shapes in the width and depth of the desk and put everything together on the floor. Or you can simply mark off the shape with masking tape. Spend some time imagining how the shape of the desk feels, and how it might be to work at this space every day. This is a good time to look at access and egress. For convenience as well as safety, staff members should be able to easily exit from behind the desk.

Support columns can interfere with furniture placement, and this can be especially challenging when any columns will be near the circulation desk location. Think carefully about how you want this handled: you want to avoid situations where columns will interfere with work that must be done at the desk, make parts of the desk inaccessible and unusable, or detract from the desk's overall appearance. A custom-built desk can often incorporate a column in the desk's design.

A variety of materials can be used to build circulation desks. Pay particular attention to the work surface, as this will receive heavy use. Laminate and linoleum are durable and economical materials to use for the work surface. If your plan calls for a reference desk, it should be in the same style as the circulation desk, so that service points can easily be identified.

A final word about circulation desks: school libraries have traditionally used circulation desks that are basically the same as those found in public libraries. Rarely has this practice been seriously questioned. It is important to remember, however, that our patrons are children and teenagers. A traditional circulation desk, with its rather formidable look and adult transaction height (often 42 inches), is not all that appropriate for K–12 students. We want to send a welcoming message to students, and this kind of desk can be intimidating, creating a barrier between students and library staff. Think about these issues when you plan a new circulation desk, particularly for younger children in elementary or middle school libraries. A circulation desk does not need to be nor should it be a monument. And there is no justification for doing something just because it has always been done that way.

Furniture for Elementary School Libraries

For elementary school children, it is particularly important to select library furniture that is designed and appropriately sized for children, not simply scaled-down adult furniture. Fortunately, more and more manufacturers are beginning to provide furniture for this market. Figures 7-17 through 7-19 show some chair and table options.

Photo courtesy of Peter Danko Designs

Figure 7-17
Body Form Children's Chair (The Danko Design Initiative)

Figure 7-18
Primaries Children's Chairs (Thonet)

Image courtesy of TotaLibra

Figure 7-19
Eurobib Tricolore Browser Table and Chairs (TotaLibra)

The primary area will include some specialized items, most notably furniture for a storytelling area. Many times a storytelling area is furnished with risers—tiered seating that is cushioned or carpeted or both—and these areas frequently are custom built. Think carefully about dimensions for tiered seating: in an informal survey of elementary schools in Massachusetts, school librarians expressed a preference for three levels of tiers, each tier 8 inches high by 18 inches deep. You can specify custom-built risers in movable sections that allow you to rearrange the storytelling area. This is an area where you can really be creative. Any number of shapes and features are possible. For example, you can incorporate storage for books, realia, or cushions. A number of products are available from furniture manufacturers for storytelling areas. As an alternative to risers, consider using stackable stools or colorful floor cushions (see figure 7-20).

The number of appropriate lounge-type seating options for elementary school libraries is limited. Rocking chairs are available in various sizes for children, and they are often quite popular with children. They can be ordered in many different wood finishes and colors.

A good solution for picture-book shelving is to specify shelf units with two divider shelves (dividers can be added to the shelves, spaced 6 to 8 inches apart) and browsing bins on the top. Another picture-book storage solution is modular cubes, which are available in wood finishes of various colors. One advantage to these cubes is their flexibility. They are easily reconfigured and allow you to combine display with regular storage.

Reading tables with sloped tops are a good table choice for elementary school libraries. Benches work well for seating at sloped-top tables (see figure 7-21).

Miscellaneous Furniture

Establish a budget for those items of furniture that may be forgotten in the planning process: book trucks, bookends, display items, shelf accessories, signage, presentation boards for instructional areas, and so on. Also, once the library has been furnished, you may want to add a few unique items, such as stuffed animals in an elementary school library, an attractive globe, or even an aquarium. Be creative!

Staff Furniture

Often the staff areas are the most neglected parts of the library. Because they may be more or less out of sight, the tendency is to skimp on the furniture quality. Keep in mind that library staff members spend all their working time in the library, much of it in work areas. You want good-quality, functional furniture. Good-quality, ergonomic task chairs are particularly important.

Floor Covering

Carpet is a good choice for school libraries. It appeals to children and teenagers, creates a warm atmosphere, is more comfortable to sit on than a hard-surfaced floor (children like to sit on the floor), helps to improve the

Photo © Peter Mauss/ESTO; courtesy of the Robin Hood Foundation

Figure 7-20

Lunella Stackable Soft Seating (M2L), PS 1 Bergen School, Brooklyn, New York

Photo © TMC Furniture, Inc.

Figure 7-21

Children's Reading Table (TMC Furniture, Inc.)

acoustics by absorbing sound, provides a safe surface, and has lower maintenance cost than hard-surface flooring. Unless your library has an entrance from the outdoors (in which case you will want the entryway floor in an easy-to-clean material: tile or some type of hard surface), there is no reason not to use carpet throughout the library, although one exception may be the library workroom. Because the carpet will get a lot of wear—and carpets are not replaced often in schools—it should be of the best quality you can afford and should be both antistatic and antimicrobial. It should also have a moisture barrier backing to prevent mold growth. Consider using different colors of carpet to designate different areas of the library and to define traffic lanes. But keep in mind that this may limit your ability to change the arrangement of areas or furniture in the future.

Modular carpet (carpet tile) is an alternative to broadloom, and it offers some distinct advantages: installation (and removal) is less expensive; it can be installed without adhesives; areas that wear faster because of heavy traffic, or places with permanent stains, can easily be recarpeted; and borders and accents are easy to create. Regardless of what manufacturers may claim, the seams of carpet tiles are visible; it is best not to try to duplicate the seamless look of broadloom. Instead, select tiles that have patterns and textures that enhance the look of a tiled floor. Before you choose modular carpet, visit some installations to evaluate the appearance.

Concerns have been raised about carpet and health and indoor air quality issues. No scientific evidence exists to support claims that carpet aggravates allergies. In fact, when carpets in public buildings in Sweden were replaced a few years ago with hard-surface flooring to reduce allergies and asthma, studies showed that occurrences of allergy and asthma problems increased dramatically.[6] Carpet traps airborne allergens, whereas hard surfaces allow allergens to remain airborne. Maintenance (keeping floors dry and clean) and materials used in manufacturing and installation are key issues. Carpet requires frequent vacuuming using vacuums with microfiltration bags; hard surfaces require frequent washing with lots of clean water to prevent contaminants from being spread around. When selecting flooring material, ask for information on emissions from the manufacturer. You should also ask for low-emitting adhesives. Obtain care and maintenance guidelines from the flooring manufacturer, and do your best to see that the guidelines are followed.

Use of Color

Colors chosen for a school library can enhance or detract from how it functions and how it succeeds as a learning environment. Because colors affect learning behavior, making suitable color choices is important; it can also be quite complicated. How and why colors affect us is a whole field of study in itself, but knowing some basic principles of the use and psychological impact of color can help you make more informed choices.

Red, orange, and yellow are considered warm colors, which tend to initiate activity. Blue and green are cool colors, which tend to have a restful, calming effect. Much of what we know about how color affects us comes from the work of the late Faber Birren, a leading researcher and writer on color. Birren found that white, buff, or ivory walls are emotionally sterile and tend to cause glare and eyestrain, and that soft colors, such as blue and yellow, induce a pleasant feeling that tends to deepen and lengthen people's concentration.[7] Lighter tones of any color will create a more spacious feeling than darker tones. Using a variety of complementary colors will create an interior that is more interesting than one that is basically monochromatic. In a review of research relevant to school library facilities, Carol A. Doll refers to a discussion of color written by Margaret Bush:

> Red, orange, and yellow can work well as accent colors, but tend to be too powerful if they dominate the environment. Instead, blues and greens are suggested as main colors. Especially important, Bush found evidence that an environment can be too stimulating. Young users in a new children's area (brightly decorated with red, orange, and yellow) were quite active physically. It was reported that the children were not as interested in selecting books to check out as they had been in more subdued surroundings.[8]

Doll further suggests that "warm yellows, peaches, and pinks can work well for children, while young adults tend to respond better to blues and greens. Too many bright, vivid colors seem to be overly stimulating."[9]

Some color choices will likely be made without your input, particularly the color of any building material that will not be painted. The architect or interior designer should create a color palette for your perusal, with samples of any item that will be used to add color to the library: floor coverings, window treatments, wall and ceiling paints, furniture fabrics and finishes, and accessories. Colors chosen should complement one another, and keeping samples together on a small scale will help you see the overall effect.

Be particularly careful with color selection for a distance learning classroom or television studio. Certain colors do not look good on camera. Before making color decisions, view color samples on video.

A Final Word about Furniture Selection and Evaluation

How can you make certain that the furniture selected for the library will last as long as it must? Here are three steps to ensure the selection of durable furniture:

1. Ask the manufacturers to supply you with warranty information, performance data, and service records. If they are unable to do so, you probably don't want the furniture item.

2. Ask for references so you can contact libraries that have the furniture. This is the best way to ascertain how furniture holds up to heavy use.

3. Obtain samples of chairs and tables. Manufacturers should be willing to supply a sample of those items you are considering. Put them through rigorous testing of your own. Don't be gentle—do everything kids will do! Kick the tables, climb on them, lean on the chairs, and sit on the backs. Ask students and staff members for their opinions. Your goal is to choose furniture that not only is sturdy and attractive but that your future users will find appealing.

Because the furniture you choose for your library will greatly affect the overall atmosphere, it is worth fighting for attractive, comfortable, high-quality furniture. What message do we give students when the interiors we provide are dull and unimaginative? That message, as Jonathan Kozol, the award-winning writer and education researcher, says, is this: "In the eyes of this society, you don't matter all that much; we don't really expect that much of you, so we're not going to waste money on you."[10] When building a new library, schools have the opportunity to show their commitment to education and to give students the message that they are valued. This opportunity should be seized.

NOTES

1. American Association of School Librarians and Association for Educational Communications and Technology, *Information Power: Building Partnerships for Learning* (Chicago: American Library Association, 1998), 142.

2. *Adolescents Read!* (January 2006), http://www .publiceducation.org/pdf/Publications/High_School/ Adolescents_Read2.pdf.

3. Keith Curry Lance, Marcia J. Rodney, and Christine Hamilton-Pennell, "Powerful Libraries Make Powerful Learners: The Illinois Study" (Canton: Illinois School Library Media Association, 2005), http://www.islma .org/pdf/ILStudy2.pdf.

4. Pauline H. Anderson, *Planning School Library Media Facilities* (Hamden, CT: Library Professional Publications, 1990), 194.

5. Matthew A. McGovern, "Oh, My Aching Back!" *School Planning and Management* (October 2000): 14.

6. Werner Braun, "Scientific Data Dispels 'Urban Myths,'" *School Planning and Management* (May 2003): 22.

7. Coleman Lee Finkel, "Meeting Facilities That Foster Learning," *Training and Development* (July 1997): 36.

8. Carol A. Doll, "School Library Media Centers: The Human Environment," *School Library Media Quarterly* (Summer 1992): 227.

9. Ibid.

10. Cheri W. James, "Congress Should Help to Modernize Public Schools," *Roanoke Times and World News*, May 23, 1998, p. A9.

8

Creating a Comfortable Interior
Lighting, Acoustics, Mechanical Design, and Ergonomics

Just being in the library makes you want to study more, and it just feels so comfortable.

—High school student,
San Francisco, California

This observation from a high school student is supported by research: the level of comfort in the work environment affects the quality of the work done there. If a comfortable library makes students want to study more, it stands to reason we would want to design a comfortable environment that will enhance, rather than detract from, the type of work activities for which it is intended. This chapter discusses four design elements that must be carefully planned to ensure optimum comfort levels: lighting, acoustics, mechanical design (heating, ventilating, and air conditioning), and ergonomics. These elements are usually not given the attention they deserve, and, because they are so highly specialized and technical, planning is frequently left entirely to the architects and engineers. All too often, the result of poor planning for lighting, acoustics, mechanical design, and ergonomics becomes apparent only after the new facility is occupied. And then, resolving problems is costly, if not impossible. The school librarian overseeing the design of a new school library facility must have a basic understanding of these elements and must be vigilant to ensure that they are well planned.

Lighting

Lighting has long been a key environmental issue in schools. In a 1986 article on the common pitfalls of library building programs, Robert Rohlf states, "The area in which most mistakes are made in library planning is lighting."[1] Eric Rockwell, in his article about the "sins of architects," notes, "Lighting in most libraries ranges from marginal to atrocious."[2] These and similar statements, heard repeatedly at professional conferences and found frequently in the professional literature, attest to the fact that lighting may well be the number-one problem in library design. Lighting systems for new school library facilities are often overlooked by school librarians and underemphasized by architects. Because we now know that lighting affects people both psychologically and physically, and that the quality of light affects performance and the quality of learning, we must pursue the goal of achieving a high-quality lighting design for the school library.

School libraries must accommodate a variety of activities, each of which requires different types of lighting and different amounts of light. Although this has always been true to an extent, it has become much more evident as the role of the school library has changed and expanded. Designing a lighting system to accommodate properly all the activities that take place in a school library is both complex and expensive. Lighting in a school library must not only provide sufficient illumination for conventional activities, such as studying and reading, but also be appropriate for computer use. Frequently, but mistakenly, a single kind of lighting, usually whatever has been used throughout the school, is considered sufficient for the entire school library.

Often, no one advocates for proper lighting. Although it is natural to assume the architect and, especially, the lighting engineer should know what kind of lighting is needed for a school library, such an assumption can lead to trouble. Lighting expert Peter Murphy, addressing the problem of lighting in school facilities, states, "It's not surprising that the quality of the final lighting solution often depends on how effective its advocate was during the construction planning and specification process."[3] For the school library, this advocate must be the school librarian, the person most knowledgeable about the function of the library and the types of activities that will take place within its walls. Murphy goes on to explain, "All too often, unfortunately, the loudest voices are those of the construction/contracting team members, who will walk away once the project is completed."[4] And because they do walk away, they don't suffer the consequences of poorly planned lighting systems. The students and staff members do.

As with other aspects of the planning process, prior planning is key to successful lighting. The planning documents needed for a new facility must address lighting requirements. By no means should you be expected to fulfill the role of a lighting consultant or engineer; you should, however, know where lighting is needed and what purpose it will serve. Architects frequently show a preference for highlights and architectural lighting. Such lighting might enhance architectural features and benefit the overall look of the space, but it will do little for the functions of the facility. It is important to insist that the lighting be designed to fit each particular function, but first we must understand some basic lighting concepts.

Lighting Fundamentals

Lighting is classified into two categories, natural (or daylighting) and electric. Contemporary school libraries are usually designed with natural light sources, such as vertical windows, clerestories, skylights, or a combination of these. As a result of escalating energy costs as well as ever-increasing research supporting the positive effect of natural light on student achievement, the use of natural light is being emphasized more and more in new school construction. Natural light, however, is affected by several variables: the direction of incoming light, the time of day, and weather conditions. Because of these variables, natural light must be supplemented by electric light for optimal performance of indoor tasks. Because school facilities are used mostly during daylight hours, there may be a danger that natural light will be given too great a role in the lighting plan.

Electric light can be introduced into a space in three ways: directly, indirectly, or a combination of the two. Direct lighting systems aim light downward into the space. Indirect lighting systems direct light up to ceiling level and reflect it back down into the space.

Direct lighting systems are very efficient at delivering light to work surfaces. However, they direct light into a space unevenly, with high levels of light directly under the luminaires (light fixtures) and lower levels of light to the sides. To compensate for this, the number of luminaires is increased, resulting in both higher energy costs and an increase in heat production. Direct systems also cause glare on computer monitors, work surfaces, and paper and can create harsh shadows.

Indirect lighting is considered to be more effective than direct lighting for overall illumination in libraries. It distributes light more evenly, requiring lower lighting levels (because visual acuity improves with indirect lighting) and virtually eliminating glare and shadows. "Researchers have found consistently that spaces illuminated with indirect lighting systems are reported to cause less eyestrain, visual fatigue, and fewer headaches than direct lighting."[5] Indirect lighting is more expensive and can be used only with a ceiling height of at least 9 feet 6 inches, and preferably more than 10 feet, although energy savings and the need for fewer luminaires will help to offset these additional costs. To provide proper illumination, indirect lighting requires a white or very light-colored ceiling. When ceiling height precludes the use of indirect light, a well-designed combination of direct and indirect lighting, with a well-shielded direct component, is preferable to direct lighting alone.

Keep in mind that any lighting system, if poorly designed, will not only create illumination problems—it will likely make the most beautiful interior look wretched. And once a lighting system is in place, problems are difficult, if not impossible, to remedy.

Lamps and Foot-Candles

Different types of electric lamps (the architectural term for bulbs) are available: incandescent, fluorescent, and high-intensity discharge (HID). Incandescent lamps are not very efficient and have a short life span; they should be used only for special situations. HID lamps (which include mercury vapor, sodium vapor, and metal halide) require time to warm up to full output—as much as thirty minutes—and to cool off. When a lamp is turned off, a full start-up cycle is required to turn the lamp on again. If the architect proposes HID lighting, ask questions about the start-up time, and ask why this type of lighting is being proposed. Fluorescent tube lighting, especially T5 (these are very bright and should only be used in indirect lighting systems) or T8 linear lamps, is the best choice for general illumination in terms of energy efficiency, lamp life, and color rendering. (The numbers refer to the diameter of the tube: the larger the number, the larger the diameter.) All fluorescent lamps require some mercury content, but lamps with reduced mercury content are available.

Fluorescent and HID lamps require ballasts—small transformers that raise voltage levels high enough to activate the lamps. Old-style magnetic ballasts can be noisy (lots of hum) and can cause lamps to flicker. Electronic ballasts used with new fluorescent lamps eliminate or greatly reduce these problems, and electronic ballasts save energy. Ballasts with a sound rating of "A" are the least noisy.

Lamps have a color rendering index (CRI), which refers to how accurately they reproduce colors. Ask for lamps with a CRI rating greater than 80. Lamps also have color temperatures that range from cool to warm. The higher the number, the cooler the light. The selection of color temperature is basically an aesthetic choice, but you should ask for an explanation of what is proposed.

The amount of light required is another factor you must consider and plan for. How much light is needed depends on the activity for which illumination is required. The amount of light present on a surface is usually defined by a uniform measurement called a foot-candle (Fc), or the foot-candle's metric equivalent, lux.

Recommended light levels for visual tasks can be found in architectural and engineering standards, such as those published by the Illuminating Engineering Society of North America (IESNA). The following are some foot-candle recommendations for various tasks:

Reading and study areas:	30–60
Computer use areas:	20–30
Service desks:	40–50
Stack areas:	30
Staff workrooms:	50
Small-group study rooms:	30–40
Multipurpose rooms:	30–50
Instructional areas:	30–70

Although it may seem that the best approach is to uniformly light all library spaces to a high foot-candle standard, the energy costs of such a plan would be prohibitive. The energy costs of an overall illumination of 80 foot-candles would be twice that of an overall illumination of 40 foot-candles. Furthermore, it is almost impossible to provide uniform light in a space that contains a combination of shelving, reading, and work spaces, as all school libraries do. It is also important to remember that too much light can cause as much fatigue as too little light. By defining the tasks to be performed in various areas of the library, proper light levels can be determined. Computer software is available that takes variables, such as ceiling height and color, into consideration and then calculates illumination from the planned system design. Require that this type of lighting analysis be done, and that any problems—areas that are too bright or too dim—be rectified.

Other Critical Lighting Issues

When lighting is being planned for the school library facility, you should pay particular attention to several critical issues. Ask the architect and lighting engineer to explain how the following issues are being dealt with in the lighting plan.

STACK AREAS

Planning effective lighting is particularly difficult for stack areas of the library. We've all used stacks where the lighting is dim, glaring, or inconsistent. Frequently it is difficult to read book spines on lower shelves. The ideal lighting plan would provide uniform illumination to all shelves, but this ideal is difficult to achieve. Stacks create shadows, and it is difficult to predict exactly how this will affect the lighting. Placing luminaires perpendicular rather than parallel to stacks will help to reduce the shadows caused by people standing at the shelves. Light fixtures that attach to the tops of book stacks are available (these must extend at least 12 inches into the aisle to be effective) and might need to be considered when it seems that stack lighting will be a significant problem. Wiring for this type of lighting can be expensive. And illumination of an area that depends on this type of specific lighting, rather than general lighting, limits flexibility. If exterior windows are located near stacks, placing the stacks perpendicular to the windows will bring natural light into the stacks. Finally, consider that shelving, especially tall shelving, affects the distribution of light throughout the space. Lighting engineers commonly overlook this effect.

STUDY AREAS

Indirect lighting in areas with very high ceilings can sometimes fail to provide sufficient illumination to tabletops. And if such areas require daylight to supplement the electric light, illumination problems will worsen at night or on overcast days. If the lighting plan poses this potential problem, you may need to purchase study tables with attached task lighting fixtures. Keep in mind, however, that if sufficient illumination of an area of the facility depends on light from table fixtures, you are limiting flexibility. If you do purchase table fixtures, they must have durable (as tamper-proof as possible) switches or switches controlled from a remote location, because students will tend to play with the switches. Avoid single-pedestal fixtures; double-pedestal fixtures are much more durable. Pedestals with additional outlets will enable laptops to be plugged into the base of the fixture. Ask questions about wiring options: wiring brought to the fixture through a track in a table leg is preferable to an electrical box on the floor under the table.

GLARE

Glare should be avoided because it creates visual stress and headaches and may eventually lead to vision-related health problems. At its worst it can be blinding and can cause damage to books. A low-glare lighting design should be a high priority, and the lighting plan should be designed to use diffuse, rather than direct, natural light. There is much controversy surrounding the use of skylights: aside from the fact that they are prone to leakage, they can present serious glare problems that, depending on the design and orientation, are very difficult to control. On the other hand, the quality of skylights has improved, and skylights with light filtering controls are available. Some skylights are designed to reflect incoming light rather than bring light into the space directly. Don't accept skylights without asking lots of questions; if you must have skylights, insist on the best quality your budget will allow and avoid locating them in areas where computers will be located and where book stacks will be placed. Clerestory windows are an effective way of bringing in glare-free natural light from the roof level and are generally a better choice than skylights.

Pay particular attention to the effect of light sources, both natural and electric, on computer monitors. Computer screens are especially susceptible to glare. Natural light either in front of or behind a computer monitor will cause glare and washout problems. Direct electric light will reflect off the monitor screens. Computer areas are best lit with indirect systems; if indirect luminaires must be used, they need to be equipped with aluminum parabolic louvers optically designed to limit brightness for computer environments.

Whiteboards are also susceptible to glare and reflection, but supplementary lighting, such as a track system, can mitigate the problem. A track system will give you more control over illumination, because you can direct light where it is needed most and in a way that will reduce or eliminate glare. Supplementary lighting also gives you the flexibility to dim or turn off any overhead lighting that may cause glare on the whiteboard.

INSTALLED COST

Before making a decision on lighting, ask about the total cost (purchase price plus the cost of installation). Systems differ in their ease of installation. Because labor can be the biggest cost element in a lighting system, a more expensive system that is easy to install may actually cost less than a lower-priced system that is difficult to install.

MAINTENANCE

Inquire about energy costs (keep in mind that some low-cost lighting systems can come with very high maintenance costs), the cost of lamp replacement, the ease of lamp replacement, and how easy or difficult the luminaires will be to clean. A luminaire may be beautiful to look at, but if it requires undue effort to clean it or replace the lamps, it will be a constant source of irritation. Resist luminaires with shades or lamp covers that students might be tempted to use as waste receptacles. Besides being a nuisance, this can be a safety hazard. For table-mounted fixtures, you don't want the lamps to be easily replaceable, or you may find yourself frequently replacing missing lamps.

CONTROLS

Pay close attention to the kind of lighting controls (switches) planned and the placement of the controls. Poorly planned controls can make life miserable. Light controls should have a simple design and be easy to operate. Controls should not be publicly accessible, yet staff members should be able to access them easily. If it is not possible to locate controls away from public areas, keyed access is a preferable option. Make certain that controls will not be placed on walls where shelving is planned. Compliance with the Americans with Disabilities Act (ADA) requires that lighting controls be no more than 48 inches above the finished floor.

Avoid energy-wasting all-or-nothing lighting: some areas of the library—instructional areas, for example—may not require lighting throughout the day. Although separate rooms should have separate controls, located inside the room at each entrance, a master switch should enable all areas to be darkened simultaneously.

Dimmers for fluorescent lights are more affordable than they once were; they provide energy savings and will help you to regulate the amount of illumination by adjusting levels as needed. Dimmers are especially useful in instruction areas where lights are positioned over projection screens, whiteboards, video monitors, and so on. Especially if the library will have abundant sources of natural light, you should consider dimmers to keep illumination even and to save on energy costs.

SECURITY AND NIGHT LIGHTS

Security lights operate when regular lights are turned off or during power outages and should provide clearly lighted entrance and exit paths. They should not be placed where they can interfere with the use of projection screens, because dimming or extinguishing lights for projection will activate the security lights. Night lights should be placed at entrances so the first person to enter the library or the last person to leave does not have to do so in total darkness.

SAFETY

Seismically active areas must have lighting engineered to withstand earthquakes. Engineering test reports are available from the manufacturers of lighting systems. As a general safety and security measure, avoid overly dim illumination for any areas of the library.

FLEXIBILITY

Avoid task-specific lighting—directing light to exact locations where it is needed for specific purposes—as this precludes flexibility. (Study tables with attached lighting fixtures might be one exception.) An architect may try to convince you that a circulation desk will never be moved. Ask yourself if you can say with absolute certainty that, over a span of forty years, there will never be a reason to move a circulation desk.

WINDOW TREATMENTS

Control of natural light using window treatments is essential for any window that does not face north. Windows should have draperies, blinds, or screens. Be wary of vertical blinds: they are an inexpensive option, but because the strips move easily, they can create irritating noise and can trigger motion-sensitive security alarm systems. Solar shades that filter heat gain, glare, and UV rays, but also let in some natural light and allow for visibility to the outside, are an effective and attractive option. Solar shades are not the most economical solution upfront, but they save energy and reduce stress on the facility's cooling system, and they are more hygienic than other window treatment options. To eliminate noise from outside, avoid placing windows in distance learning classrooms or audio/video production areas. If there are windows in these areas, they must have treatments that allow for complete control of sunlight.

* * *

Developing the lighting plan is a cooperative effort, and it is one area where you will need to rely on the expertise of others. Let the architect know early in the process that you want to be included in the planning for lighting. When that time comes, request a meeting that includes the lighting consultant, if there is one, and the lighting engineer. If you have properly defined where and for what purposes lighting is needed, you can discuss options within the scope of the budget. Make sure the lighting plan is coordinated with the plan for heating, ventilating, and air conditioning (HVAC) systems, because light—both natural and electric—creates heat. Finally, because colors look different in different kinds of light, try to use the same light planned for the space when you are selecting the colors of finishes and fabrics.

Acoustics

Acoustical concerns in library media centers are much more important and complex today than they were in the past. Years ago, before electronic resources were such a vital part of the library environment, we had only to deal with noise produced by people. Today, the widespread use of computers, printers, and other equipment has added machine noise. People noise has also increased, because group work and instruction are essential parts of the instructional process; the modern school library is no longer the quiet zone it once was. Yet libraries must still provide quiet for study and reading, because many of our students need and want a quiet study environment. Because of these changes in learning and teaching styles and in school library functions, it is now much more important to address acoustics in the planning process, to anticipate problems, and to design spaces where unwanted noise can be eliminated or at least kept to a minimum.

Because acoustics are typically not a code requirement, they can easily be overlooked during the planning process, and problems will only become apparent when you move in. Acoustical engineering is a complicated science; by no means can school librarians be expected to know how to optimize acoustics. It is important, however, that you know something about acoustics— what to avoid, some solutions to problems, and, perhaps most importantly, what questions to ask.

The larger the space, particularly when it has a high or vaulted ceiling, the more difficult it is to achieve good acoustics. Because we tend to want school libraries with large, open areas that provide flexibility, we must deal with spaces that present acoustical problems. Where possible, design fully enclosed rooms for activities where noise is generated or where quiet is preferred. Staff workrooms, offices, conference rooms, and group instruction areas are best planned as separate rooms with floor-to-ceiling enclosures. Because voice-activated computer technology is likely to become commonplace, consider separate areas for some computer workstations; if supervision is needed, select partitions with a sufficient number of windows to allow for visual control.

The most effective way to provide enclosed spaces and still maintain flexibility is to use wall systems rather than fixed walls. Wall systems, which consist of wall panels (with glass for visual control) and door units, are more expensive than fixed walls, but they can be moved and reused. Prewired power and data options are available, which can cut down on wiring costs. They are also available with a variety of acoustical options. In the main library space, try to place zones with comparable noise levels adjacent to one another. Shelving can help separate these areas from areas where quiet is desired by acting as a buffer to reduce noise transmission.

In addition to the size and shape of a space, acoustics are affected by the kinds of surfaces and textures in that space. Hard surfaces, such as tile, stone, and glass, will not absorb sound and, therefore, will contribute to sound reverberation and a noisier space. In the school library, especially in those areas where noise is undesirable, it is best to avoid using these hard surfaces. Carpeting, fabrics, textured wall treatments, and acoustical ceiling tiles will all help to absorb sound. If maintenance concerns require a floor covering other than carpeting at the entry, circulation area, or other high-traffic areas, consider using resilient flooring. Acoustical panels can be attached to wall surfaces and can enhance the appearance of the room when designed with an appropriate motif. Acoustical treatments can also be suspended from ceilings over areas needing noise reduction: sound baffles hang vertically, and sound panels in a variety of sizes and shapes (often referred to as "clouds") hang horizontally.

Noise from adjacent spaces within the school building, such as cafeterias, music rooms, and gymnasiums, can also present acoustical problems. Find out what spaces will surround the library and be above and below it. If any of these spaces will be noisy, ask what measures will be taken to keep this noise from affecting the library. If the school is located in a noisy area, near heavy traffic, for example, ask for double- or triple-glazed windows with high STC (Sound Transmission Class) ratings that will prevent noise from entering the library. Be sure to ask about the location of the building's mechanical systems. The noise and vibration generated from these systems should be kept to a minimum within library spaces. Potential problems from noise generated by mechanical systems are often overlooked. Any adjacent mechanical rooms must be equipped with sound barriers to isolate noise and vibrations. Television or audiovisual production and recording areas must also have special acoustical treatment.

Noise Criteria (NC) rating is a standard that describes the relative loudness of a space. The lower the number, the quieter the space. Because speech intelligibility is an important consideration in school libraries, NC ratings should be used. Ask for the following NC ratings for specific areas of the library:

Reading, study, and instructional areas: NC 30 or lower

Circulation and reference areas: NC 40 or lower

Teleconference or distance learning classrooms: NC 25 maximum

For instructional areas, consider the use of infrared amplification technology. This will benefit all students and is especially important for students with hearing impairments and for boys, whose hearing is significantly less acute than that of girls.

Do not hesitate to ask questions. As you review plans, ask specifically what acoustical treatments are being planned for the library and how they will be implemented. If you anticipate acoustical problems, and if the architect is not addressing your concerns, find out if he or she will consider consulting with an acoustical engineer. Remember that it is far less expensive to design acoustical solutions into the project than it is to remedy problems once construction is complete.

Mechanical Design

Most states report inadequate heating, ventilating, and air conditioning (HVAC) systems as key environmental problems in schools, and in today's school design much attention is being paid to indoor air quality. It is impor-

tant for school libraries to have proper HVAC systems not only for the health and comfort of staff members and users but also for the safety, operation, and preservation of materials and equipment.

Because a school library houses an expensive inventory of materials and equipment and may operate outside scheduled school time, it should have a separate, independent HVAC system. An independent system will permit use of the library during nonschool hours and will maintain temperature and humidity levels for proper storage of materials and equipment at all times.

Consider the following when planning mechanical systems for school libraries:

Temperature control. The Library Administration and Management Association standard for materials is a 12-degree variation from 65 degrees year round. "Studies have indicated that the best temperature range for learning is sixty-eight to seventy-four degrees, and that the ability to learn is adversely affected by temperatures above seventy-four degrees."[6] We must, therefore, consider the students, not just the books. And since a majority of students prefer and learn better in warm rather than cool temperatures, care must be taken that the facility not be overly air conditioned, especially in warmer southern climates.

Humidity control. Relative humidity levels should be maintained between 40 and 55 percent (40 percent is optimal for computers). Relative humidity levels above 60 percent will cause damage to materials and present health concerns. Levels below 40 percent will cause materials to dry out and disintegrate and cause static electricity to build up. The mechanical system should be designed to maintain this relative humidity level even when the library is unoccupied and other heat and air conditioning systems are off.

Supply and return air vents. Vents should be located in such a way that people will not be in drafts and papers will not blow away. Vents should not create undue noise, especially in production and recording areas and in distance learning classrooms.

Fresh air. At least eight to twelve changes of air should take place per hour.

Operable windows. The ability to manually open and close windows helps provide adequate ventilation.

Because wall space is frequently needed for shelving in school libraries, components of mechanical systems should not be installed on or in front of walls. Components should be placed high enough not to interfere with furnishings.

Ergonomics

The discipline of ergonomics attempts to design a work environment that prevents job-related injuries, improves worker health and comfort, and increases operational efficiency and effectiveness. Most ergonomic research has focused on adults; very little has focused on children or teenagers. This lack of research, along with the fact that students are not generally thought of as "workers," has contributed to a lack of attention to ergonomic issues in schools, and controversy over the topic is a result. Some experts argue that children are not prone to musculoskeletal disorders, while other experts believe children might be more prone than adults to such injuries. Existing research fails to conclusively substantiate either opinion. What is known and now almost universally accepted is that furniture used in schools needs to be comfortable and appropriate for the task, and provide good support.

In the past, while schools rushed to install computer hardware, ergonomic concerns were overlooked, and little if any attention was paid to providing comfortable and appropriately designed furniture for students. If you look at pictures of library furniture in catalogs, on websites, and in journals—even pictures of award-winning, exemplary interiors—you will easily find examples where comfort was not given proper consideration. There are far too many newly designed school libraries in which students' legs dangle from chairs or won't fit under work surfaces, and computer monitors and keyboards are placed in such a way that heads and arms are bent at awkward, unhealthy angles. This situation is beginning to change; today there is more demand for comfortable, ergonomically designed furniture for schools, and furniture manufacturers are responding. Unfortunately, many architects, interior designers, and school furnishings consultants are still specifying, and many schools are still buying, furniture that is based on decades-old designs.

Anecdotal reports indicate that as little as one hour per day working at a computer may put the user at risk for musculoskeletal injury. Because of the varied nature of school librarians' work and the nature of students' work, the risk of such injuries is certainly not as great as it is for someone doing data entry eight hours per day. Risks do exist, however, and planners should be required to consider ergonomics when selecting furniture for the school library. Because students spend more and more time at computers, both at home and at school, they may well be at risk of developing the same kinds of work-related injuries and long-term health problems known to affect adults. Comfortable and appropriately designed furniture can influence a child's well-being and task performance, and considering ergonomic issues when purchasing furniture may help to prevent injuries and health problems in students.

How can we address this issue properly and apply what is known about ergonomics to school libraries? There are no easy answers, and the nature of children and adolescents presents special problems. We can help students establish good ergonomic habits—especially the importance of changing position every fifteen to twenty minutes—and select furniture that will keep children and adolescents comfortable and will promote proper posture.

We must exercise a great deal of caution when evaluating furniture in terms of ergonomics. There is no standard definition of ergonomic design and, as a result, no real accountability. When we select furniture for a library, we are selecting it not for one specific person, but for many potential users, and these users come in many sizes and shapes. There is no ergonomically correct furniture for all situations and all people. This is especially true for school libraries, where the same furniture will be used by many different students and many different age groups. The key, therefore, is to select furniture that can be easily adjusted and—particularly in elementary and middle schools where there is a significant size difference among students—to avoid purchasing furniture that is all one size. Some specific dimensions to follow when selecting ergonomically correct furniture were listed in chapter 7. Here are three additional guidelines:

Chairs for computer workstations should have medium-height backs that are slightly concave vertically. Back angle (forward/backward position) should be adjustable (a lever adjustment is more durable than a handwheel adjustment). Seats should have a waterfall front (this relieves pressure on the back of the thighs), and the height should be adjustable (a pneumatic cylinder adjustment is the most durable) so that a user's feet can be placed firmly on the floor.

Keyboards should be just below elbow height when arms are bent at a 90-degree angle: approximately 23 to 28 inches above the floor. They should be flat or have a slight negative tilt, with the back edge tilted down and away from the user. For young children, consider keyboards designed to fit smaller hands. If you purchase furniture with adjustable keyboard trays, they must be sturdy and wide enough to accommodate a mouse and mouse pad.

Positions of monitors should be adjustable to allow for a distance of at least 18 inches away from the user (or at about arm's length), and for eye level at 2 to 3 inches below the top of the monitor.

When selecting adjustable furniture for student use, keep in mind that students have a natural tendency to play with adjustments. Although this is a nuisance and can contribute to premature breakage of the mechanisms, it is not sufficient reason to avoid adjustable furniture altogether; we must learn to deal with it. Consider carefully your own situation; decide which adjustments are most important, and look for adjustment mechanisms that are easy to operate and durable enough to withstand frequent student use.

* * *

Because the fields of lighting, acoustics, mechanical design, and ergonomics are so technical in nature, you and other members of the planning team may believe that decisions concerning these aspects of the design process are best left to the architectural team. Taking this course of action is a huge mistake and will almost certainly result in a facility that has some significant failures. Not only must you be involved in this phase of the design process, you must also take the initiative, as it is unlikely your opinions will be solicited. Carefully written statements that define activities and delineate your needs will help the architect plan according to your requirements. Asking questions and monitoring the process will help to ensure that your needs are met. Lighting, temperature and humidity, acoustics, and ergonomics all affect the behavior and performance of the library's occupants. Your goal should be to seek solutions that will provide the most comfortable environment the budget will allow.

NOTES

1. Robert H. Rohlf, "Library Design: What Not to Do; Successful Library Building Programs Avoid These Common Pitfalls," *American Libraries* (February 1986): 101.

2. Eric Rockwell, "The Seven Deadly Sins of Architects," *American Libraries* (April 1989): 341.

3. Peter Murphy, "What You Need to Know about Classroom Lighting," *School Planning and Management* (April 1999): 1.

4. Ibid.

5. Paul N. Grocoff, "Electric Lighting and Daylighting in Schools," *CEFPI IssueTrak* (December 1995), http://www.cefpi.org/issue1.html.

6. Michael E. Hall and Stephen J. Wilczynski, "Student-Centered Sustainable Design," *School Planning and Management* (July 2005): 24.

9

Creating a Green Interior
Sustainability

In recent years the design and construction fields have seen an increasing interest in constructing and furnishing buildings in a way that has a minimal impact on the environment. If the benefits of building green are important to you, you may need to provide a voice like that of the Lorax in Dr. Seuss's story that chronicles the plight of the environment. And even though yours may be a limited voice in terms of methods and materials used in construction, it can be a catalyst for change. It is worth having at least a basic knowledge of the topic and knowing how to look for and suggest materials and furnishings for the school library that are environmentally friendly.

First, it is good to be familiar with some of the "green building" terminology. These terms are closely related and are often used interchangeably, but they do have distinct meanings.

Green. Products that are naturally friendly to the environment are referred to as green. Methods to produce materials and buildings are referred to as green if resources are used in ways that are not wasteful.

High-performance. High-performance buildings are buildings that are superior in a number of ways, particularly with regard to energy efficiency, maintenance costs, site disturbance, indoor environmental quality (IEQ), durability, and adaptability. High-performance schools have these superior qualities and are designed to help teachers teach better and students learn better.

Recyclable. Recyclable materials are or can be reused rather than disposed of. A floor covering made from used rubber tires is an example of a recyclable material.

Renewable. Renewable resources do not deplete the natural environment; they can be produced as fast as they are consumed without destroying the original source. Wool and bamboo are examples of renewable resources.

Sustainable. Materials that are sustainable are acquired in ways that are environmentally sound; sustainable methods do not compromise the health of the environment or the health of a building's occupants.

When constructing a new school facility, adopting principles of green building design can provide the community with a learning laboratory and will help to achieve the goal of making the educational experience healthier and more productive. Although constructing a green school building requires additional planning, and initial upfront costs may be higher than with more conventional construction, cost savings occur over the life of the building through reduced energy costs and fewer maintenance requirements. It is reasonable to assume that improved indoor environmental quality keeps students and staff healthier and, therefore, may reduce absenteeism; because school funding formulas are often linked to average daily attendance, this would result in increased funding. The benefits of building green have prompted some states to offer financial assistance specifically for the construction of high-performance schools.

California was one of the first states to encourage the building of high-performance schools and to enact stringent guidelines: the Collaborative for High Performance Schools (CHPS). A number of other building guidelines have been created for schools, including the U.S. Department of Energy's EnergySmart Schools Initiative and programs provided by the Sustainable Buildings Industry Council.

Established in 2004, the U.S. Green Building Council's Leadership in Energy and Environmental Design (LEED) program has become the national standard for green building design. The LEED Green Building Rating System provides a specific set of guidelines and uses a scorecard to measure building performance. To achieve LEED certification, a facility must meet minimum standards in six areas of building design:

Sustainability of site

Water efficiency

Energy and atmosphere

Materials and resources

Indoor environmental quality

Innovation and design process

A project must earn a minimum number of points across these categories to be LEED-certified. Schools across the country have now achieved LEED certification.

Even though the school building project you are involved with may not be seeking LEED certification, there are still a number of levels of sustainability that can be made part of the design. And the area where the school librarian can have the greatest environmental impact is the selection of library furniture; the school librarian can make this a goal even if the rest of the school project does not follow suit.

Although the benefits of sustainability are difficult to dispute, some words of caution are in order. A manufacturer may make environmental claims, but such claims can mean any number of things. For example, a manufacturer may claim to be a green company, but this may simply mean that the company has a paper recycling policy. If a manufacturer makes an environmental claim, ask for documentation. Also ask for any third-party certification that requires independent assessment, but be aware that such certification can be expensive. A small company may not be able to afford the expense of certification, but the lack of certification does not automatically mean the company's environmental claim is dishonest. If a product has a certification label, determine exactly what that certification means: GREENGUARD certification, for example, specifically concerns emission standards and air quality levels. Remember that manufacturers want to sell their products, and their claims can often be confusing or misleading. Ask lots of questions before accepting what you are told.

The school library has some unique furniture requirements among which durability is paramount; this is especially true of shelving and seating. Some furniture that has green certification, or is in other ways friendly to the environment, may not be sufficiently durable for library use. The furniture may thus have to be replaced sooner, which defeats the purpose of buying green. Select a green product over one that is not when all other selection criteria (including product warranties) are met and equal. In the end, perhaps the most environmentally sound approach is to purchase furnishings that will last as long as possible.

10

Making the Library Accessible

An Inclusive Approach

If we practice what we profess, namely, that we want to invite, welcome, and encourage all students to use school libraries, then we should take to heart the words of one of the key figures of German literature and design school libraries to be as accessible as possible. This chapter discusses ways in which we can achieve that goal. First, it covers requirements established by the Americans with Disabilities Act (specifically those that are of concern when planning new or renovated school libraries). Next, the chapter deals with signage and learning styles. Finally, some issues concerning safety are discussed.

Americans with Disabilities Act

Signed into law in 1990, the Americans with Disabilities Act (ADA) is a comprehensive civil rights law that prohibits discrimination on the basis of disability. Titles II and III of the ADA mandate handicapped access to public facilities. The intent of the law is to ensure that facilities are accessible to and usable by people with disabilities by making those facilities barrier free. The Access Board (originally the Architectural and Transportation Barriers Compliance Board) is responsible for developing accessibility guidelines (ADAAG) for newly constructed and renovated buildings. The initial guidelines were issued in 1991. The ADAAG provide guidance to the Department of Justice, which is responsible for enforcement of Titles II and III of the ADA. Noncompliance is treated as a form of discrimination. The Access Board may from time to time amend the ADAAG, and the Department of Justice may amend its own regulations that implement the ADA by adopting these new accessibility guidelines.

The original accessibility guidelines were based on adult dimensions and did not include children's dimensions even for facilities designed for use primarily by children. In 1986, the Access Board recommended accessibility guidelines for children with physical handicaps in elementary schools. These recommendations were developed to assist states in designing and constructing accessible elementary schools. Many states have applied these recommendations to newly constructed schools serving grades 1–6. New accessibility guidelines approved in July 1999 provide further options based on children's dimensions as exceptions to specifications based on accepted adult dimensions. These optional specifications are discretionary, not mandatory, and they focus on certain elements designed and constructed primarily for use by children age 2 through 12.

Much confusion exists about many aspects of the ADA, and it can be difficult to interpret. Architects do not always know all the rules. Because it is a complex law, any school undergoing a new construction or major renovation project must rely on experts to be certain the provisions of the law are met. The school's contract with the architectural firm should specify that the new facility must be ADA compliant. It is also important to know that some states have accessibility requirements more stringent than the federally legislated requirements.

School librarians involved in building projects must have a basic knowledge of ADA requirements in order to ask intelligent questions and to monitor progress with respect to the ADA. Becoming familiar with the relevant provisions of the ADA is well worth your time and the time of everyone involved in the building process. If barrier-free design is not incorporated into the plan at the beginning of the process, additional costs will be incurred down the road.

To understand ADA requirements, you must be familiar with certain principles and definitions upon which they are based:

According to the ADA, an adult wheelchair needs clear floor space 48 inches deep by 30 inches wide. Because actual dimensions of wheelchairs vary, be aware that this space may not always be adequate, especially for some motorized wheelchairs.

Any reach above 5 feet or below 20 inches is not accessible to a person in a wheelchair.

To make a right or left turn in a wheelchair, a space 36 inches by 36 inches is needed; to make a smooth U-turn, the space needed is 78 inches by 60 inches. (The space requirements to make a U-turn need to be considered when shelving alcoves—shelving that dead-ends at a wall—are part of the furniture plan.)

You should be aware of several ADAAG requirements that have specific application in libraries:

Entry and all interior doors must be at least 32 inches wide. Thresholds must be beveled with a thickness of no more than ½ inch.

Door hardware must be operable with one hand, with no twisting of the wrist required, and must be mounted no more than 48 inches above the finished floor.

A user of a wheelchair must be able to enter and exit through any theft-prevention system, or an alternative entry and exit must be provided.

Any library on more than one building level must have elevator access available for all levels.

Floor surfaces must be smooth and covered with firmly fastened, nonslip materials. Carpeting must have a hard pile ½-inch maximum thickness) with a firm, stable, and slip-resistant finish, and it must have a firm or no-cushion backing or pad.

Accessible routes must connect all spaces within the library. These routes, including aisles between book stacks, must be at least 3 feet wide. The ADAAG express a strong preference for a 42-inch aisle, and a 48-inch aisle at the end of a range of book stacks is preferred. If your library is designed with the minimum space between stacks, pay particular attention to exact shelf dimensions. A shelf with a depth of 10 inches may take up more floor space than 10 inches, and end panels may extend beyond the dimension of the shelf.

At least 5 percent, or a minimum of one of each element, of fixed seating, tables, and carrels must comply with ADAAG requirements. This applies to all public areas of the library. Accessible routes must lead to and through these areas of seating. Clearance between tables and carrels must be at least 36 inches. When planning areas of lounge seating, clear space should be made available to accommodate users of wheelchairs.

Floor space at a table or workstation must be a minimum of 30 inches wide by 48 inches deep. Only 19 inches of the depth is allowed to be underneath the work surface.

Knee space beneath a work surface must be at least 27 inches high, 30 inches wide, and 19 inches deep. For children age 12 and younger, the minimum height is 24 inches.

Where wheelchair seating space is provided, work surfaces must be 28 to 34 inches above the finished floor. For children age 12 and younger, the minimum height is 26 inches. Consider the use of some height-adjustable tables or carrels to meet this requirement (see figure 10-1 for one example).

Clear aisle space at displays of periodicals, new books, and so on must be at least 36 inches; maximum reach height must be no more than 54 inches from a side reach and no more than 48 inches from a front reach, with 48 inches preferred irrespective of approach. Book-stack heights are unrestricted.

The circulation desk must be on an accessible route. The desk must have a countertop that is at least 36 inches long and a maximum of 36 inches above the finished floor. If students are checking out materials and are required to sign their name or write something, you must have a surface no higher than 34 inches, with knee space so a wheelchair can fit under it.

Liquid Workpace Table photo courtesy of Bretford

Figure 10-1

Height-Adjustable Table (Bretford Manufacturing, Inc.)

The maximum height for placement of light switches is 48 inches.

If the bottom edge of an object that protrudes into a passageway is more than 27 inches but less than 80 inches above the floor, the object must not protrude more than 4 inches into the passageway.

In addition to becoming familiar with the ADA, perhaps the best way to make the library free of barriers is to consult students with disabilities. Ask them what features would be most useful in a new library facility. The ADA guidelines often fall short of true accessibility, and it is important to remember that these guidelines are minimum, not optimal, requirements. The minimum 36-inch accessible route guideline, for example, may be barely sufficient for children. Children in wheelchairs may not be as skilled in operating them and may need more room to maneuver than adults need. Increasing the amount of space for accessible routes does, of course, add up to a significant amount of extra space needed for the facility. Increasing the space between shelves from 36 inches to 42 inches, for example, requires 1.5 square feet more space per shelving unit, which translates into additional dollars. This additional space is worth fighting for, however, as is designing for as much accessibility as you can afford.

Signage

Signage is an integral part of the interior design of a school library. Too often it is either ignored altogether or overdone, creating visual clutter that defeats the purpose.

Planning

Signage should be planned along with the design of the library facility and the selection of furnishings. Some designers recommend that signage not be planned until after the new facility is occupied, the argument being that traffic patterns and usage can then be better observed. In theory this is a good idea, but dangers accompany this approach. First, good-quality sign systems are not inexpensive. The best way to guarantee a good system is to plan it in advance and include it in the furnishings budget; otherwise, finding the necessary funds later may prove difficult or impossible. Second, the wait-and-see approach often results in a haphazard system of signs that are handmade, look makeshift, and spoil the library's appearance. If you choose to wait and plan signage after the facility is finished, do so only if you have a guaranteed budget at your disposal.

The signage for a school library is not as complicated to plan as that for a large public or academic library. Not many signs are needed, and, if you've planned for a natural traffic flow, it will be clear where signs will be the most helpful. The sign system you purchase should be one that can be updated or modified easily and economically, and it should be portable, not permanent. The signage plan should be coordinated with the lighting plan, so light fixtures hung from the ceiling do not obscure any signs.

The planning for a sign system should begin when you are visiting other libraries to get ideas for your new facility. During these visits, take note of what you like or dislike about the signage. Catalogs and websites from companies that specialize in signage will give you some idea of the range of available products.

The purpose of signage in the school library is to help users navigate and make it easier for them to find what they need; this removes psychological barriers and makes the library more inviting to the user. The format, color, and type style should be consistent, and the signs must complement the setting. Avoid clutter: if there are too many signs, they tend to become invisible.

Common Signs

The signs most commonly needed in school libraries identify the circulation desk, the areas of the collection (fiction, nonfiction, reference, periodicals, and so on), and the range of books found in each shelf unit. Range finders will most likely need frequent updating, so it is very important to purchase signs that can be easily changed in-house. Range finders commonly have protective covers over the labels, and the covers can be secured with screw-type locks to prevent tampering. These covers should have a matte finish to avoid glare. Consider including some signs in lay language to identify subjects within the nonfiction collection (ask yourself why bookstores don't use the Dewey Decimal System).

Terminology

The terminology for signs should be based on common sense and should be easily understood and meaningful to everyone. Use action words when appropriate, and avoid professional jargon or terminology that may be out-of-date in the future. If your library has a reference desk, consider identifying it with a sign that says Ask a Librarian; for the circulation desk, consider using the terms Checkout and Return, or Customer Service. Give the terminology some thought, and solicit ideas and opinions from students and teachers. Be creative and maybe just a bit daring.

Once you've decided your terminology, be consistent: use the terminology not just throughout the facility, but for all library information, including your library's website. Try not to be boring; don't think it always has to be done the same old way.

Design Elements

In addition to signs, design elements can help users find their way in the library. Changes of color on the floor, for example, can be especially effective to designate traffic lanes and functional areas. Different colored shelves can help to distinguish types of resources: reference, nonfiction, and fiction. Again, be creative. One elementary school library very successfully used objects to identify nonfiction classifications: a baseball mitt for sports, a toy truck for transportation, a suitcase for travel, a stuffed animal for mammals, and so on.

ADA Requirements

Signage must also meet ADA guidelines (and any existing state or local building codes), and your specifications should require ADA compliance:

Permanent rooms and spaces must be identified with signs. These signs must have tactile lettering (a minimum of $1/_{32}$ inch thick). Lettering must be between $5/_8$ inch and 2 inches tall and must include grade 2 braille. Permanent room signs must be mounted on the same side of the door as the door handle, 48 to 60 inches from the center of the sign to the floor. If a door opens out, the horizontal center of the sign must be placed 9 inches from the edge of the door.

All permanent, directional, and identification signs must have a nonglare finish and sharp contrast between the colors of the letters and the background.

All overhead signs must have letters at least 3 inches high and must be hung a minimum of 80 inches above the finished floor.

Learning Styles

Teaching methods have changed considerably as a result of scientific research that has helped us better understand the brain and learning. And yet many newly designed school facilities fail to reflect this knowledge. When a new or renovated school library facility is planned, it is important to apply what we know about the brain and learning to the design process. The new facility should provide an effective learning environment, one that supports different learning styles and enhances the learning process. As Ross Todd notes, "The school library is no longer a warehouse space, but rather, a learning place."[1]

Exactly what constitutes an effective learning environment will vary from school to school and will depend upon the age group the school serves as well as the size of the facility and number of staff. How the school library will reflect our knowledge about learning will be determined to a large extent by the planning documents and by the educational specifications these documents outline. To ensure that it will effectively support the school's educational program, the library program must be carefully thought through and clearly defined.

Consider the following specific learning style issues when planning the school library interior:

Some students learn better in a quiet atmosphere; others learn better with low-level background sounds or music.

Some students learn better in bright light; others learn better in soft, low light.

Most students learn better in warm temperatures; some learn better in cool temperatures.

Some students learn better with formal, traditional seating; others learn better with informal, more comfortable seating.

Some students need to work alone; others need to work in groups of two or three.

Some students learn better when they are allowed to have food or drink while studying; all students need to drink water throughout the day to remain hydrated.

To stay focused, adolescents need to move even when seated; what adults refer to as fidgeting and slouching is often an expression of this need.

Remember that these are needs that enable students to learn and perform better; they are not frills or preferences.

Perusing school library websites, one finds an overabundance of school library rules such as these:

Please whisper. If you need noise to work, find another place to work; the library is a place for those who want to work quietly.

All activities will be conducted in a quiet manner.

No more than four students per table.

No food or drinks are allowed in the library. Eating and drinking must be done outside the library. Food and drinks will be confiscated and you may be asked to leave.

No bottled water allowed.

Sit up straight.

Many consider these rules in keeping with appropriate library use, and the adults who implement them may be well-meaning. But such rules are not consistent with a welcoming, inviting environment, they contradict what is known about the learning process, and they do not contribute to a school library that is accessible and appropriate for all learners.

This is not to suggest that all rules be abandoned and that we allow anarchy to prevail. But we must rethink the past, when educational facilities were designed more to manage students than to enhance the learning process. And though it is not practical or even feasible to provide the optimum learning environment in the school library for each and every student, providing options is key—as many as possible and far more than we have provided up to now. In the past (and too often today), school library facilities were designed to treat everyone the same, as though everyone learned in the same way. This practice must not continue; it is time to question old assumptions and effect positive change.

What are some options that deserve consideration as we plan and design environments more conducive to learning? Consider providing the following:

Quiet-only study areas.

Study areas where music is playing in the background, or where personal audio devices are allowed.

Study areas with different levels of light.

Controls that allow temperature variations in study areas.

A variety of seating options, including formal seating, comfortable seating, areas for individual study, and areas for small-group study (see figure 10-2).

A place within or adjacent to the library (at least at the high school level) where selected food and drinks are allowed, even if only at certain times during the school day. Some school librarians will consider this suggestion heresy. But there are many success stories of school libraries with cafes and coffee shops, and librarians in these schools report increased circulation and improved reading scores as a result. Food and drinks do not need to be allowed throughout the library, and clearly restrictions need to apply to areas where computers are located. What's key is that a library cafe should not serve merely a social function, but should exist to complement learning.

When designing for learning, it is again the role of the school librarian, as well as other school personnel, that is critical. Do not assume architects and interior designers are familiar with how people learn or with changes in how schools function today compared with ten or more years ago. That assumption is why we see new school library facilities that are designed on an outmoded educational model. This is why you must be involved. Remember, we want all students to use school libraries. Although there is no guarantee that students will use library facilities that offer environments conducive to their learning styles and needs, it is unlikely they will choose to use library facilities that do not.

Figure 10-2
Small-Group Study Room/Lounge Seating

Safety Issues

Provisions for the safety of students as well as library staff members should be included in the planning process. Location of the library within the school plays a role in safety. The library should not be tucked away in some remote corner from which a quick and easy evacuation is difficult. How the library is designed in terms of supervision is also critical. The shape of the library should be such that no spaces are hidden from view. Stacks should be configured to facilitate supervision of aisles, and staff work areas must include windows so a staff member can supervise outside adjacent spaces. The use of glass in walls that are adjacent to corridors is one of the easiest and most effective means of making the library a safer space.

The correlation between facility size and capacity and number of staff is a safety issue that needs to be recognized—often it is not. A large facility cannot be effectively supervised by one person even if that person can see the whole library clearly. One adult supervising a hundred or more students in a library is inherently dangerous.

Local building codes will usually determine how some safety issues must be addressed. Meeting these codes is the responsibility of the architectural firm. The ADA also has guidelines for safety features that must be met. Some of these safety issues, including floor covering, protruding objects, adequate aisle space, and furniture design, affect accessibility and have been covered earlier in this chapter. The school library should be equipped with an alarm system that is both audible and visual. Varying or intermittent tones are recommended over steady tones because they are more likely to be heard by persons who are hard of hearing. Alarms must be at least 80 inches above the floor and at least 6 inches below the ceiling. Because the requirements specified by the ADA for alarm systems are very technical, it is important that the company that supplies the system guarantee compliance with existing laws. Emergency exits must be provided as well as exit signs and lights.

Once the facility is complete and ready for use, you must have an emergency management plan, and any such plan must address the needs of the disabled. Being prepared for an emergency is probably the most important step to take in terms of safety. Evacuation procedures must be clear to users of the library so they can act quickly, and staff members must be fully prepared to implement emergency procedures.

Our school libraries serve a diverse mix of students, and our goal should be to design library environments that all students can use effectively and easily. When planning a new school library facility, you should try to go beyond mandated or minimum requirements. The principles of universal design, which attempt to make the built environment usable by as many people as possible, are worth following. The more inclusive we can make our school libraries, the more they will benefit everyone.

NOTE

1. Ross Todd, "From Information to Knowledge: Managing the Infoglut and Leading School Reform" (NEEMA Leadership Conference, Moakley Court House, Boston, MA, March 3, 2006).

11

Buying What You Want
Specifications and Bid Documents

There is hardly anything in the world that some man cannot make a little worse or sell a little cheaper; and people who consider price alone are this man's lawful prey.
—John Ruskin

The words of John Ruskin, the art, architecture, and social critic, point to the importance of not relying on cost alone when selecting furniture and equipment for school libraries. And though cost is certainly an issue that must be considered, Ruskin believed that a thing is worth what it can do for you. The least expensive item will be worthless if it does not do what you need it to do.

Most public schools must follow a competitive bidding process when ordering furniture and equipment for a new school library facility. Even if competitive bids are not required, the procedure is often worth following. The amount of furniture and equipment required to furnish a new school library is substantial, and competitive bids will almost always yield the best volume discounts. Sometimes the bid process can be bypassed by ordering items from state or other educational pricing contracts, when such contracts exist and when the desired items are included in the contracts. This is a tempting option because it eliminates the writing of specifications, but it will not guarantee the best prices. A number of documents make up the total bid package, including specifications for all items to be purchased. A carefully prepared bid package will enable you to buy furniture and equipment that will meet your needs and hold up to heavy use.

If your library facility is part of a larger building or renovation project, it is best to have a separate bid package prepared for the library media center. This is a common practice, because library furniture requirements are significantly different from and more complex than requirements for classroom and other school furniture. For example, although generic shelving may be suitable for a classroom, it will not be suitable for the library. You may need to make known—early in the process—your opinion that a separate library bid is the preferred procedure.

You can find help with preparing specifications through several sources. You can hire a library building consultant to prepare specifications. A large building project may warrant hiring a project management firm or an individual project manager to oversee and coordinate the process and take responsibility for preparing specifications. If your school district has a purchasing department, there may be someone on staff experienced in specification writing who can either prepare them for you or at least assist you in the process. If you find yourself involved in writing specifications, a good place to begin is with manufacturers. Identify furniture and equipment that meet your criteria, get detailed specifications on the items from the manufacturers (many manufacturers now offer product specifications online), and build your specifications around them. You can also ask for copies of specifications from other schools that have done this before and use them as a guide.

When someone else prepares the specifications and bid documents, you must still be involved. When the school library media specialist is not involved or doesn't know what to look for, things can, and often do, go wrong. A case in point: shelving 10 inches deep for the fiction and nonfiction collections was specified by the planning consultant for a new middle school library; when the bid documents were prepared by the architect's furniture planner, the shelving depth specifications were changed to 12 inches. The result: not enough room for the total number of shelving units planned and an overall shortage of sixty shelves—storage for some 1,500 volumes. This case points to the necessity of inspecting documents at each and every stage. You must check, double-check, and triple-check. For most of us, this is time-consuming, boring detail work, but it is extremely important.

To oversee the writing of specifications and preparation of bid documents, you need to understand what a bid package is, what specifications must include, and how the process works. A bid package consists of three basic parts: the requirements for bidding, the specification of items, and general conditions. The requirements for bidding will usually be a standard procedure already in place that the school uses for any bidding process. Your concern is with the specifications and general conditions.

Specifications

Specifications tell the prospective bidder what will be purchased. The method of writing specifications can be categorized into two basic types: generic specifications and one-manufacturer specifications.

If your goal is to obtain specific models from specific manufacturers, the one-manufacturer procedure is best. Only by specifying a particular product can you be assured of receiving exactly what you want. Using this method is easier, because it eliminates the need to compare various products in terms of quality, a task that is difficult if not impossible. Also, all bidders bid on the same specific item. For most furniture and equipment, competitive bids can be obtained for the same item from three or more distributors. A variation of this procedure is to allow vendors to bid on an item of equivalent quality rather than the item specified; however, it is important that they ask you for approval before they make substitutions, and you should require that the vendor provide a sample of the equivalent item so you can evaluate it. You can also give more options to bidders by listing more than one acceptable model and manufacturer for any given item. If you use this method, be certain to include a basic description of each item. Using model numbers alone can result in problems: typos occur easily, and often model numbers for identical products can vary from vendor to vendor.

Most schools prefer to use generic specifications, which describe an item (the specifications may be based on one manufacturer's product), but do not identify a specific manufacturer. With this procedure, detailed specifications are critical. (An example of item specifications is shown in appendix F.) Some manufacturers build knock-off versions of other manufacturers' products that can look identical to the originals but may be of lesser quality. It is not unheard of for bidders to disregard some of the specifications. Because such things can and do occur, bids submitted in response to generic specifications must be very carefully reviewed.

With either the one-manufacturer or the generic procedure, it is best to put items into sections or groups. This is essential if, for example, a chair you want is not available from a distributor who can provide the kind of shelving you prefer. For a typical school library, furniture groups would include shelving, tables and carrels, seating, service desks, signage, and miscellaneous (book trucks, display items, file cabinets, etc.). Arranging specifications into groups allows a vendor to bid on one particular group. A bidder is not required to bid on every group. However, the bidder should be required to bid on each and every item within a group. Bidders should be required to give unit cost as well as total or extended cost for all items bid, which will make comparison of submitted bids easier. The bidder should also be required to give a unit price for any additional quantity purchases beyond those listed in the bid. This will eliminate having to negotiate the price if you decide to order a few items over the quantity stated in the specifications. Bidders should be asked to quote a price that includes inside delivery, assembly, installation, cleanup, and removal of packaging materials.

General Conditions

General conditions include when, where, and how bids will be accepted; the contractor's obligations for delivery and installation; the owner's right to inspect items; procedures for damaged pieces, shortages, delays, failure to fulfill the contract, and acceptance of work; insurance requirements; your right to request samples and performance testing; guarantees; and terms of payment. Conditions should require all bidders to verify all measurements to ensure proper installation and to be responsible, at no extra cost, for any modifications needed at the time of installation.

Before the bid package goes out, you should ask to review it. This is the time to check that everything is as it should be. Pay particular attention to the specifications listed for each item as well as the quantities. Make sure quantities match what is reflected on the furniture plan. Check that all items of furniture and equipment ordered are included.

Sometimes a pre-bid conference may be scheduled at a time after the bid package goes out. This gives potential bidders the opportunity to ask any questions they may have concerning the content of the package. This can save a lot of time and confusion, and it is a recommended practice, although you may need to suggest it.

If you have a preferred vendor, you should inform that vendor as soon as the project has gone out to bid. This may be the only way the vendor will hear about the request for bids, and it is the best way for you to ensure that the company will submit a bid before the specified deadline.

It is difficult to time delivery exactly right. Delivery dates will be based on the expected completion date of construction work, but that date is always subject to delays. The bid package should hold the vendor responsible for any required storage of items received before a delivery date. The bidder should also be instructed to provide the estimated time required from receipt of the order to delivery. For most furniture, plan on at least twelve weeks. If you need delivery and installation during the summer, allow additional time; this is the busiest time for manufacturers and vendors of educational furniture. The bid process itself can take three months or more; a distributor needs sufficient time to prepare quotes (two to four weeks), and you need time to analyze submitted bids and determine the successful bidder. These time allowances mean a bid package must be ready for bidders at least five to six months before delivery is required.

After vendors have submitted quotes, all bids received are compared, and the successful bidder chosen. You must be involved in this process. Choosing a successful bidder is as important as hiring an employee; you and your library users will have to live with the decisions made now for many years to come.

Contrary to popular belief, it is not a requirement to automatically award a bid to the lowest bidder. In fact, accepting the lowest bid can be very shortsighted; a low price may mean the vendor is offering poorly manufactured, lower-quality materials. Conversely, the highest-priced bid does not necessarily guarantee the best outcome. Bids should be awarded on the basis of overall value. Cost is only one of several criteria on which to base a decision. Most importantly, generic specifications must be compared with the items a vendor submits in the bid package. Bids that do not meet specifications can be eliminated. The reputation of the bidder should also be considered (including financial stability and length of time in business). Ascertain the reliability of vendors by asking for and checking references before the bid is awarded. Check on overall satisfaction with meeting delivery and installation deadlines, the quality of installation, and the willingness and ability to resolve problems satisfactorily.

Keep in mind that in general, a detailed bid package with requirements thoroughly spelled out should result in fewer problems, and it is better to have specifications that are too detailed rather than too vague. A bid package is a legal document, and you should not attempt to put one together by yourself. No one should expect you to do so. But do be involved in the process from beginning to end.

12

The Final Phases

Construction, Delivery, Installation, and Moving In

Once construction of the new facility is under way, and vendors for furniture and equipment have been chosen from the bid process, it may seem that the time has come, at long last, to sit back and exclaim that all your hard work will result in a library media center that "rocks." And although it is true that the end is in sight, and you may indeed feel that you deserve a rest, this is not the time to step out of the picture. There are still important details that require your attention, and failure to stay on top of what is happening may allow mistakes to go unnoticed, undoing the diligence you've practiced up to now. In the final phases, you must continue to stay alert and be involved. This chapter focuses on the last few steps in the process of creating your new library.

Construction

During the construction period, it is important to monitor progress. This is a delicate proposition. You want to be certain that work is being done properly (don't assume it will be), but you don't want to be viewed as someone who is interfering. If it is possible to visit the construction site, arrange to do so. Try to arrange at least two such visits. Know the chain of command, and arrange any visit through proper channels. Don't just wander onto the site. This is dangerous and probably illegal, and it will make you very unpopular with the contractor and construction crew.

Before visiting the construction site, review and familiarize yourself with the architectural plan, and take a copy of the plan with you. Be prepared to check for the overall shape of the facility and placement of walls, doors, windows, electrical outlets, data connections, and switches. If something does not appear to be right, bring it to the attention of the person in charge (it may be the architect or, if there is one, the project manager). It is best not to question construction workers, and under no circumstance should you ask them to make any changes. They are following instructions and have no authority to make changes you might want. Your role at this stage is to monitor the progress of what has already been planned. If the planning was done properly and thoroughly, you should not need to request changes unless a mistake is being made or a serious error will result. Changes at this stage of the process are usually costly.

If you have ever been involved with house construction or renovation, you already understand the importance of monitoring construction. It is not uncommon for the architect, project manager, or contractor to make changes once construction is under way, and you are not likely to hear about such changes. In most cases, the changes will be minor and will not affect the outcome in a negative way. But mistakes can be made, and it is not unheard of for a wall to appear in a place where it does not belong.

Once construction is complete, punch lists are prepared after the architect and a school representative carefully inspect the project. The punch lists will detail things that need to be completed or corrected before the facility can be considered finished. When these items are satisfactorily done, and after a certain waiting period, the school will sign off on the project. Before this occurs, you should obtain a complete set of "as-built" blueprints for the library facility. These drawings indicate construction details that differ from the original plans. It is essential to have these plans for future repairs and alterations. You should also organize all warranty information, noting when warranties expire. This will facilitate the process of inspecting items before the warranty expirations.

Delivery and Installation of Furniture and Equipment

When deliveries and installations are scheduled, be on the site: this is an absolute priority. When something goes wrong, and some things almost surely will, resolving problems after the fact is much more difficult. Do not let anyone convince you that your presence is not necessary.

Delivery and installation of furniture and equipment should not be scheduled until all building tradespeople have completed their work and no longer need to be on the site. (There is one exception: to ensure that data and electrical connections are placed properly for any furniture that needs to be hardwired, cable and electrical installation workers will need to complete

their work at the same time that furniture is installed.) If furniture is in place while interior work is still being done, the furniture will be used and possibly abused. Damage may result, and it will be a challenge to hold anyone responsible.

The delivery and installation process will probably take two or more days, depending on the number of distributors involved. Even though it will lengthen the process, it is best to schedule deliveries so you only have to deal with one distributor at a time. If possible, develop a plan for delivery and installation that will allow larger items (especially shelving and service desks) to be installed first, and smaller, more easily damaged items last. This will help to eliminate, or at least minimize, any damage from moving furniture into place.

On delivery days, have copies of the furniture plan available, both for you to check and for installers to follow, as well as copies of all relevant orders. Ask in advance if the distributor plans to send a representative to supervise delivery and installation. If this is not planned, see if it can be. The most obvious task is to verify quantities of items delivered against quantities ordered and to report any shortages. You must also check every item for damage. It is almost inevitable that some damage will have occurred in shipping or will occur in the process of installation. Often damage will be only minor nicks and scratches, and the installers can make repairs on-site. But you need to note all damage and make certain that it is properly repaired before final acceptance is given.

Some adjustments, especially of wall shelving, may need to be done on-site. Even if all measurements were accurately taken, construction is not always exact. Shelving must be installed in straight lines and be level and stable. Wall shelving should be anchored securely to the wall. There should be very little movement or swaying of shelving units. Reject any argument that shelves will stabilize once books are in place. If empty shelf units are not stable, they'll most likely be even more unstable (and more dangerous) when fully loaded. Tables and chairs, too, should be level and stable.

Installers should treat furniture carefully. Don't let anyone put tools or equipment on furniture, and see that the installers protect carpet from dirt or damage. When installation is complete, all items should be clean and all debris and packaging materials removed from the site.

Moving In

Most new school library facility projects, and probably all renovations, will require moving materials, equipment, and furniture either from storage or from the old facility to the new facility. This is a tedious job, and it needs attention to detail. You need to develop a step-by-step plan for moving that will fit the requirements of your specific situation. The plan should include procedures for removing items from the existing location as well as procedures to ensure proper placement of these items in the new facility.

The easiest and most effective way to move is to hire a firm that specializes in library moves. Unfortunately, this is also the most expensive way, and most schools simply cannot afford it. If a professional move is not a possibility, you will need to come up with creative solutions. If you are located near an institution of higher education that offers a library science program, look into hiring some library school students to assist with moving. They will bring to the task an understanding of library organization. If no funds can be made available, the move will have to be carried out by school personnel and volunteers. Don't have more people helping with the move than you can adequately supervise. And once the move is under way, be aware of safety issues: you don't want anyone injured in the process. As with everything else, you can benefit from other people's experiences. Ask for suggestions from other school librarians who have had to move facilities, and search the Web and online databases for recent articles on relocating library collections. Incorporate what will work for you into your plan.

Print materials will likely be the biggest challenge in moving. Books are heavy, there are lots of them, and they need to be moved in a way that will keep them in reasonable shelf order. This is a good time to seriously weed and clean. Get rid of anything that is no longer useful. If your move does not involve much distance, and if you haven't had to put books in storage, it may be possible to eliminate the need for packing. You can load books on book carts and simply wheel them to the new facility. Some schools have organized human chains from the old location to the new, with books being passed from one person to the next. If you need to pack books, it is important not to overload boxes. One box per shelf is usually best. Boxes should be clearly labeled on all sides, so you can always determine the contents of a particular box. Devise a labeling system. For example, you can use a color or letter for the different sections of the collection and assign numbers for the shelves within each section. Boxes should also be marked as belonging to the school library. Sturdy boxes of uniform size will make for a smoother move. If possible, purchase boxes from a moving company rather than collecting boxes of various sizes and strengths. Boxes with precut handholds are much easier to lift and move.

For other boxed materials and items, as well as equipment and any existing furniture that will be moved, devise an identifying system, but be careful how you mark any items that will not be boxed. (Any tape or other adhesives should be easy to remove without damaging the item.) Then, on the floor plan of the new library, indicate where these items should be placed. You want to avoid a situation in which everything moved is simply dumped wherever there is space.

Ideally, the move will occur when school is not in session. However, if your move must take place while school is in session, your plan should allow you to continue operating the library with as little interruption as possible. Be realistic, and allow yourself the time required to make the move.

Celebrate

The construction is complete, you've moved into the new facility, and you are ready to begin library operations in that facility. Now you can put your feet up, give a sigh of relief, and remember what your life was like before all this began. All your hard work has paid off, and you can feel proud of your success. Some type of celebration is in order, even if it is just a personal one! Some schools will organize official dedication ceremonies; others will have some kind of open house. It is best not to schedule a celebration for the public immediately after moving in. Give yourself a few weeks to get properly unpacked, settled, and familiar with your new surroundings. Whatever you choose to do to celebrate your success, be certain to at least publicize the wonderful features of your new facility to teachers and students. Feature your new facility, with pictures, on your library website. You put so much effort into planning this new space, it only stands to reason you will want everyone to know about it and benefit from it. Also, consider hosting some kind of open house for other school librarians in your area. We can all benefit from seeing new school libraries and from hearing about the experiences, both good and bad, of planning and designing a new facility.

13

Combining Facilities
Joint School-Public Libraries

Do not go where the path may lead, go instead where there is no path and leave a trail.
—Ralph Waldo Emerson

The American writer and philosopher Ralph Waldo Emerson believed that all of life is an experiment. And though combining school and public library facilities may still be considered experimental, success stories of combined school and public libraries are accumulating from a number of countries. This may be an experiment worthy of consideration. There are some outstanding examples of successful joint libraries, particularly in smaller communities—communities with fewer than 10,000 residents. In the 1970s there were 84 joint libraries worldwide. By 1992 that number had more than doubled, to 199.[1] Currently 40 percent of public libraries in Sweden, 40 percent in South Australia, 8 percent in Canada, and less than 2 percent in the United States are joint facilities. Some are true joint facilities, and others are adjacencies. And though most ventures have taken place in rural or low-population centers, with today's focus on creating small communities within urban settings, we are beginning to see a trend in joint libraries in urban areas as well.

If the community is willing to explore the possibilities, schools in communities where collegial relations exist between the governing bodies may want to consider crafting a joint library with their public library. A library of this type does not mean a branch of the public library housed in the school, or just a repository for resources, but a joint-use public-school facility that would simultaneously serve both the school and the public communities throughout the day and evening. Although not a solution for everyone, a joint venture is a possible solution for a community in which neither the school nor the public library is meeting its potential. "Your answer rests in the complex chemistry in the individual communities and their libraries studying the decision."[2]

Successful programs thrive on a spirit of collegiality rather than competition. After all, the philosophies and roles of school and public libraries are decidedly different. In "For the Public Good: Joint Use Libraries in Australia and New Zealand," Bundy includes a table clearly identifying the differing roles (see Selected Readings). There needs to exist a willingness to give up some political and operational control as boards of different governing sectors make compromises for the betterment of library service to residents and students.

In *Joint Ventures: The Promise, Power and Performance of Partnering*, the California State Library delineates the differences between partnerships and joint ventures and, in chapter 2 in a section titled "Joint Use: Libraries Plus Schools Equal Learning Success," identifies several positive examples of community pride in joint ventures (see Selected Readings).

Difficulties

Although joint ventures have been occurring more frequently over the past several years, little in the way of guidelines has been written to help develop a successful venture. Library literature is replete with failures, revealing a variety of reasons. Most often cited are a history of noncooperation between town agencies; a lack of clear governance that includes defined areas of responsibility; a lack of periodic evaluation, review, and adjustments; political conflicts between different governing bodies; and a lack of planning.

Be aware that politics can play a big part in the success or failure of the concept. Of primary concern is the ability of different legal entities to enter into a governance compact that defines the roles and expectations of the joint venture. Library staffs need to meet to develop an operational and managerial model that leads to policy and procedure development, which, in turn, leads to approval by the governing boards of the school library and the public library. In most states, the school board (or school committee) is an autonomous entity governing the school community. The library board of trustees is also autonomous and is responsible for the public library. Depending on your state's laws, additional legislation may be required to join these governing groups.

Although the town's governing board is not directly involved, its approval is crucial to the concept. In other words, it is an all-town effort, not just an effort of the school and the public libraries. The development of a governance document is an essential element in the process. The Wisconsin Department of Public Instruction, Division for Libraries and Community Learning, provides an excellent guide for the development of a joint library, along with a checklist that helps in the creation of the governance document (see Selected Readings).

Other issues of concern are intellectual freedom (open access to resources and filtering), security (after hours and concerns about children and the public),

resource ownership (discrete budgets), network ownership (technology access, consortiums, etc.), collection development, hours of operation, operational and management issues (policies, procedures, fines, multiple circulation areas, restroom access, coffee bars, etc.), and staffing patterns. Traffic patterns both inside and outside the building are important as adults can be intimidated by large numbers of teenagers or noisy children. Public library patrons cannot be asked to deal with school bus schedules or to wade through classes of young children to get to the circulation desk or restrooms.

It must be understood and accepted that establishing a joint library is not a cost-saving venture but an effort to improve services. Economies of scale and collaboration are often more than offset by operational issues of expanded programming and staffing, except in the construction and furnishing phases, where savings may accrue.

Advantages

Improved library service for students and members of the community is the primary potential benefit of a joint school-public library. Improvements include the availability of better trained staff; the availability of a richer, more diverse collection; the ability to access both collections; longer hours of operation for patrons; collection development coordination; expanded programming, particularly for young adults; and full-year use of the school collection. Social advantages to the community include intergenerational interaction; implementation of a community-wide educational entity that serves everyone; and a clear, visible "library" message to the community as shown by a shared vision and common goals. In addition, the public library is recognized as fully integrated into the educational community of the town, students see the role models of adults continuing to read and learn, and adults see the children in an instructional setting in ways not previously possible. Closer relationships develop between the community and librarians, and children witness firsthand the lifelong use of libraries. More efficient building use is an added benefit. There are some potential economic advantages as well, including shared (and therefore lower) operational expenses (utilities, HVAC, maintenance, and insurance); increased opportunities for purchasing discounts; and less space required for nonusable square footage (space for mechanical and electrical systems, telecommunications closets, stairs, restrooms, elevators, custodial functions, and other common building elements).

Another potential benefit includes significantly increased circulation. Furthermore, two entities can build one larger facility as opposed to two smaller ones. A recent project in Vermont showed that designing a separate public library required virtually as much space as did a redesigned school library expanded to accommodate a joint school and public facility. And though no one should enter this process assuming that there will be major fiscal benefits, there can be substantial economies of scale in the construction and furnishing phases. Bundy provides an extensive list of possible drawbacks and advantages in his 1999 "For the Public Good" article.

Case Study: Conceptual Design for a Joint-Use Library

If you are considering establishing a joint school-public library, you may find the following case study useful.

The community embarked on a major construction project to renovate all schools and to include a center for community activities. With a population of 7,000, and with a twenty-year growth potential of an additional 2,500, the community fell within the guidelines for considering a joint school-public library. With the library as its centerpiece, the community center would include gymnasiums, meeting rooms, and a large auditorium, creating a new Town Center for both cultural and recreational activities. Many designs were reviewed by the community governing boards as well as the residents before a final design was approved. Uppermost in the minds of community members was providing the spaces needed for current and projected programming.

The final design for the library divides the total space in two halves. One half is shared space between the school and the community center. The other half is subdivided into two separate spaces, each for exclusive use. The community is confident that the final design enables a substantial increase in the program of library services that can be offered to students and community residents. The melding of the collections will produce an opening day collection of around 50,000 volumes. Design capacity can accommodate approximately 65,000 volumes over the next twenty-year period.

Communication was key to keeping everyone informed, and all feedback was addressed by either

implementing design changes or providing a rationale for few or no adjustments. Key issues addressed included overall safety issues; the location of and separation of children's/adult restroom facilities; separation of school groups from the general public areas; separate school/public entry areas to avoid congestion; separate adult computer access without filtering; a glass enclosure for the children's area to contain noise; sightlines (low shelving) for ease of supervision; use of space outside school hours; joint circulation of merged collections; and continued ownership of resources by each governing entity. The inclusion of other meeting areas in the complex, but outside the walls of the library itself, reduced some of the pressure for additional large meeting space within the library. Exterior considerations included providing high-visibility signage for the library, providing ample parking, and routing school traffic away from the community parking areas to allow for unhindered parking access.

The layout shown in figure 13-1 illustrates the areas and adjacencies developed for the joint-use library. The overall space is approximately 16,500 square feet, roughly divided into 3,700 net square feet (nsf) public library, 3,500 nsf school library, and 8,000 nsf shared space. Because the library is located within the school facility, the requirement for nonusable square footage is only 7 percent instead of the more usual 20 percent. Public library, school library, and shared spaces are indicated on the drawing. (*Note:* Although this case study is based on a real example of a collaborative project that is still in progress at the time of this writing, the authors—who consulted on this project—made minor modifications to the final library design in order to illustrate what we believe is an optimal design solution for this project.)

The librarians will develop joint governance procedures and determine what types of scheduling will best work, how best to share and schedule some of the areas, how best to catalog and shelve the various collection segments—Young Adult (YA) fiction, YA paperbacks, Chapter Books, Reference (Quick Reference for Students, General Reference, etc.)—and so forth. For example, although the archives room will be primarily a public library space, seniors at the school will need to use the archives for required research on the community and its history. Therefore, direct supervision of students at these times will be required. A mutually agreeable procedure will be developed to handle this special need. Another example is adult access to school-owned technology resources during nonschool hours.

As figure 13-1 shows, there are basic space expectations for both the school library and public library operations. They include adequate instructional space; seminar/conference rooms (multiple, with multimedia production access); large-group meeting rooms; separate entrances, circulation desks, and restroom facilities; distinct adult areas; a story hour and activities center; teen spaces; technology (hardwired and wireless) access; an archives and historical collections area; storage; workrooms; offices; and amenities for a bakery, coffee shop, mini-store, and so forth.

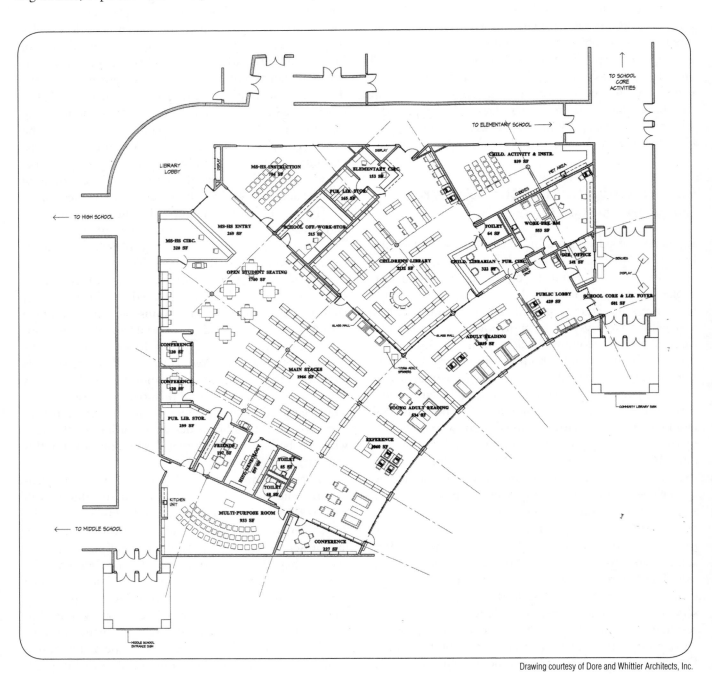

Drawing courtesy of Dore and Whittier Architects, Inc.

Figure 13-1

Conceptual Design for a Joint-Use Library

Challenges

Careful planning and good communication are key to achieving many of the benefits and meeting many if not all of the challenges of creating a joint school-public library facility. Challenges that must be considered and resolved include the following:

Securing commitment from administrators, decision makers, staff, and the public

Achieving a joint effort by two autonomous legal entities, which may require legislation

Crafting a sound governance document, with periodic reviews to enable growth and change as the community matures

Identifying start-up costs (unifying the catalog, deciding and codifying policies and procedures, providing planning time for both professional staffs, covering moving expenses, etc.)

Accepting that staff salary levels differ between the school library and the public library

Maintaining adequate funding and staffing, including staff who serve as coordinating and liaison personnel with responsibilities for cooperative activities

Being willing to share some areas of the facility and to schedule their use to benefit all users

Addressing safety issues involving young children and increased public access

Supervising more square footage with traditionally small staffs

Evaluating the joint venture on an ongoing basis as part of a continuous planning process

Keep in mind that a joint venture is not an irrevocable decision. Twenty to thirty years ahead, as the town and schools change, populations grow significantly larger (over 10,000), and new or expanded facilities are required, the joint venture should be examined in light of the trends of the time. Such an examination may reveal the need to dissolve the shared facility, and two separate entities might evolve, or it may indicate that an expanded joint facility would be of greater benefit to the town and students.

A joint school-public library is not the best answer for everyone, but for some communities, it should be part of the process of determining how to provide the very best library services for the community as a whole. It is not an overnight decision but one that takes time, effort, planning, strong commitment, and a willingness to look beyond parochial interests for the betterment of the community's family of learners. As Charles Handy states, "Those who are always learning are those who can ride the waves of change and who see a changing world as full of opportunities. They are the enthusiasts and the architects of new ways, forms, and ideas."[3]

NOTES

1. A. Reist and L. Highlander, "Joint-Use Libraries" (student project for University of North Texas School of Library and Information Sciences, Public Libraries course, February 2000), http://www.unt.edu/slis/students/projects/5320/reist.htm.
2. J. Lobner and L. Kaslon, "School/Public Library Combinations," *Nebraska Library Association Quarterly* 31, no. 2 (Summer 2000): 17–21, http://www.state.ne.us/home/NLA/nlaquarterly/2000-2-LobnerKaslon.html.
3. Charles Handy, *The Age of Unreason* (Boston: Harvard Business School Press, 1998), 58.

14

Conclusion

Building on the Experience of Others

A shy country boy who became the founding father of IBM, Thomas Watson was known for his willingness to take chances and try something new. He believed that great accomplishments result from the transmission of ideas. School librarians who have been involved in designing new school library facilities have stories and ideas to share that are worthy of our attention. We can benefit from listening to the voices of experience, taking chances, and learning from what others have learned.

One voice of experience comes from Janis Wolkenbreit, who oversaw the planning for a new high school library facility in Amherst, Massachusetts. The overall success of the facility makes Janis's comments and advice noteworthy.

The planning process began two years before the start of construction. When asked what she did to prepare for the process, Wolkenbreit says,

> I did an enormous amount of reading—everything I could find on library design and exemplary library programs. I attended every conference I could that had anything to do with library and/or school building programs. I visited all kinds of libraries.

Teachers and librarians from other kinds of libraries in the community were on the committee that prepared the educational specifications. The detailed planning for the library was not done by committee, but by Wolkenbreit herself. During that phase she communicated frequently with students and staff and solicited their ideas. A consultant was hired to assist with the planning process. Wolkenbreit found this outside help very beneficial:

> One of the main reasons was that the consultant lent credence to what I was requesting. The building committee was more comfortable that an expert supported my ideas. I had some pretty definite ideas of how I wanted the library to function and look. Having a consultant helped to refine those ideas and troubleshoot things I might not have thought of. In terms of technology, it was very helpful to have someone who knew what was really possible, instead of what was the easiest and cheapest but not necessarily the most sound.

The library has a seating capacity of 120, and at 8,800 square feet it is spacious compared to many high school libraries. Yet Wolkenbreit feels the library could benefit from additional space. She notes that although the facility can accommodate three classes at one time with room left over for individual users, it is often over capacity.

Wolkenbreit's final advice to others: "My recommendation is to talk to as many librarians as possible, look at as many facilities as you can, and talk to several furniture manufacturers."[1]

From school librarians who have gone through the process, certain words of advice are heard again and again. And though these points have been made in preceding chapters, they are worth repeating.

Involve yourself before you're asked and before something bad happens. Get involved at the very beginning. Some of the most important decisions are made very early in the process.

Try to get help. Don't abdicate your role in the process, but don't hesitate to ask for help. The complexity of the task and the enormous amount of time required can easily overwhelm you. Mistakes are extremely costly.

Don't let others make decisions best made by you. You are the school library media program expert.

Have your program define the facility. The facility is built for a specific purpose—to enable the program offered to students and faculty. Architectural motifs or designs should not impede the functioning of your program.

Don't be intimidated by the architect. As in any profession, there are good architects and bad architects. Don't mistake arrogance for competence. The architect is hired to work for you. Be positive but assertive.

Avoid the situation in which the architect gets one set of information from you and a conflicting set of information from someone else. If this happens, your information will probably be superseded. Be sure you know the channels of communication and who is making the decisions.

Don't be afraid to disagree. You have a right to voice your opinion even when it conflicts with what someone else thinks. But don't be disagreeable.

Don't always accept the first idea proposed. This is important advice even if the idea is yours. Take time to think things through carefully.

Challenge the "it has always been done like this" mentality. Designing a new facility is an opportunity to rethink traditions. Don't be afraid to innovate when it's the right thing to do.

Look at plans from a user's point of view. It's easier to develop plans from your point of view, but don't overlook how well the user will be able to function in the new facility.

Don't design just for you. We all have our own particular wishes, but someone new will someday staff the facility you plan.

Don't plan to fill every nook and cranny. Clear space is vital to the proper functioning of a facility.

Plan for sufficient storage. Where are you going to put all those boxes, supplies, and your coat? Plan spaces for library staff, and remember to ask for a sink in the workroom.

Check and double-check the location of light switches. Switches have a tendency to change locations during the architectural design process. Keep an eye on them. Will they be convenient?

Be alert for change orders made by others. Such changes may have negative consequences that cannot be undone once they are implemented.

Remember telephones. Don't assume there will be any or that they will be located where you want them.

Involve maintenance staff in the planning process. They will be responsible for maintaining the facility once it is operational, and they will look at issues from a different yet important perspective.

Plan for the future. You are planning a facility that needs to function well for a long, long time. Have a vision. Think flexibility.

Avoid designing or purchasing anything that encourages young children to run, jump, or climb. Some things that fall into this category may be visually interesting, so the architect may suggest or design them. But you don't want injuries.

Assume nothing. Assumptions usually lead to trouble. Check, double-check, and triple-check.

Keep your sense of humor. There will be times when you will be frustrated, demoralized, and angry. These are times when you need to laugh.

Paying attention to these cautions will save you a lot of grief and prevent a lot of mistakes. Copy and post this list in places where you will see it often.

Finally, it is important never to lose sight of the fact that it is students we serve. Their voices are also worthy of our attention and are frequently thoughtful and insightful. In order to attract students to our school libraries and to remain relevant, we must give their needs and wants our respect and full consideration. Remember the school library media specialist who complained that no one asked for her opinions? No one is likely to ask for the students' opinions unless you do.

In ten communities participating in the Public Libraries as Partners in Youth Development initiative funded by the DeWitt Wallace–Reader's Digest Foundation, teenagers were asked what libraries must do to change their image. "When asked to think about libraries and describe the images or color associated with libraries, young people responded, 'dark,' 'dreary,' 'gray,' 'black,' 'dull,' and 'boring.' Library furniture was described as not comfortable or the right size for

teens."[2] When asked for ways library spaces could be improved, the teens used the adjectives *bright, cheerful, welcoming, friendly,* and *exciting.* Had they been asked to describe school libraries, it is quite likely the responses from these young people would have been the same.

What can you do to make your new facility a place of learning that is a world of excitement for young people? Begin with the design. Designing means creating according to plan; the challenge is to plan an inviting facility, one that does not cling to the past but instead looks to the future. When you begin the process of designing a school library media facility, accept that challenge with enthusiasm! You can make a difference.

NOTES

1. Janis Wolkenbreit, interview by authors, Amherst, MA, November 1999.
2. Elaine Meyers, "The Coolness Factor: Ten Libraries Listen to Youth," *American Libraries* (November 1999): 44.

A

Common Architectural Symbols

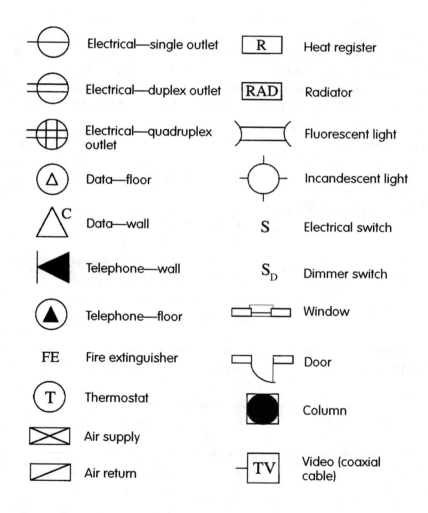

Symbol	Description	Symbol	Description
	Electrical—single outlet	R	Heat register
	Electrical—duplex outlet	RAD	Radiator
	Electrical—quadruplex outlet		Fluorescent light
△	Data—floor		Incandescent light
△C	Data—wall	S	Electrical switch
	Telephone—wall	S_D	Dimmer switch
	Telephone—floor		Window
FE	Fire extinguisher		Door
T	Thermostat		Column
	Air supply	TV	Video (coaxial cable)
	Air return		

Suggested Space Allocations and Adjacencies

The following spaces (for schools with 1,000 or fewer students) should be considered in the planning process. Some are needed by all libraries, and others are needed only when the program requires them. The square footage allocations are suggestions only and are based on recommendations found in the professional literature, on recommendations from state departments of education, and on what experience tells us works. (*Note:* Space for shelving, generally integrated into main use areas, is not included in these space allocations. See chapter 5 and appendix D for information on shelving space requirements.)

Main Use Areas

Library Space	Considerations/Relationships	Space Allocation
Entry/Circulation/Information	May include terminals for patron access to the catalog Includes space for display Copy machine in area or in close proximity Adjacent to main library entrance Adjacent to staff offices and workroom Adjacent to periodical and equipment storage	500–800 sq. ft.
Individual Reading/Study	Can be integrated into other areas of the library Locate in quiet areas Tables should seat no more than four students	Number of seats @ 30 sq. ft. each
Computing	Can be integrated into other areas of the library	35–45 sq. ft. per computer workstation
Leisure Reading	Adjacent to periodical display and display of new books Locate in easily supervised area	Number of seats @ 30–45 sq. ft. each

Library Space	Considerations/Relationships	Space Allocation
Storytelling	Adjacent to picture book collection Locate in quiet area, but where sound will not disturb other areas	15 sq. ft. per child
Group Study	Adjacent to reference area and group instruction	Number of seats @ 30 sq. ft. each
Small-Group Study and Activities	Locate in easily supervised area May have movable walls to allow for combining areas	Number of seats @ 30 sq. ft. each
Group Projects and Instruction	Accessible by groups without disturbing quiet areas Accommodates the use of all types of media	900–1,500 sq. ft. More space required if more than one class is to be accommodated simultaneously
Computer Instruction	May be included with group projects and instruction	900–1,500 sq. ft.
Multimedia Production	Provides for production of all types of media Accessible by groups without disturbing quiet areas	300–1,600 sq. ft. Allocation will depend upon the number of students the space must accommodate simultaneously
Television Studio	Designed to support viewing as well as production Adjacent to multimedia production, audiovisual equipment storage, and distance learning Must be free of ambient sound Ceiling height: 14 ft.	1,600 sq. ft.
Distance Learning Classroom/ Videoconferencing	Adjacent to television studio	1,600 sq. ft.
Teacher Resources	Provides storage for professional books and periodicals Provides access to library catalog and other electronic resources Additional space needed if a production area is included	600 sq. ft. or more depending on number of resources

Support Areas

Library Space	Considerations/Relationships	Space Allocation
Offices	Adjacent to circulation Windows to allow for visual control of the library Accommodates collaborative planning between teachers and librarians Provides storage for professional library collection	150–500 sq. ft.
Workroom	Accommodates processing & repair & storage Adjacent to circulation, offices Physical and visual access to other support and production areas Direct access to corridor is desirable Consider providing a restroom for staff	300–400 sq. ft.
Storage	Adjacent to or incorporated into workroom	400 sq. ft.
Periodical Storage	Space required depends on the collection size Availability of full-text electronic databases has reduced the need for periodical storage Adjacent to lounge seating area	150–250 sq. ft.
Non-print Media Storage	Adjacent to or incorporated into equipment storage and workroom Adjacent to circulation area	200–400 sq. ft.
Equipment Storage/ Distribution/Repair	Adjacent to non-print media storage Provides storage for supplies Work surfaces for routine maintenance and minor repair Access to corridor	400–800 sq. ft.
Equipment Closet	Must be a space dedicated for telecommunication needs Avoid proximity to large electrical equipment Requires space for file server maintenance	150 sq. ft. (minimum)

C

Sample Area Data Form

South High School Library

Area:	Library Office/Workroom
Space Requirements:	800 sq. ft.
Occupancy:	1–4 library staff
Adjacencies:	Circulation, Storage
Security/Supervision:	Visual control of adjacent general library areas
Activity Description:	Provides space for administrative work, small-group meetings and conferences, collaborative planning, production of materials needed for the library, storage of supplies, temporary storage of new acquisitions, processing of new materials, repair of materials, and the technical operation and support for information technology systems.
Additional Information:	Consider direct access to corridor.

Physical	*Environmental*
Antistatic carpet (vinyl composition tile or resilient flooring acceptable)	HVAC: Ventilation and supply, air conditioning
Windows to allow views to circulation desk and main library	
Any windows to outside will need treatments for sun control	
Nonglare lighting	
Plumbing: sink	
Walls of sound-absorbent materials finished in muted, neutral colors	
Adequate electrical outlets	
Surge suppression	

Communications	Furnishings and Equipment
Clock	Staff task chairs
Telephone	Guest chairs
Fax machine	Four-person table for collaborative work
Data ports	Counters with cabinets above and below
	Lockable coat storage
	Shelving for new acquisitions
	Shelving for professional books
	File storage
	Paper cutter
	Color laser printer
	Flatbed scanner
	3–4 computers
	Tack board

APPENDIX

D

General Information on Shelving

A. Shelving section width: 3 feet

B. Shelving heights (in inches)

1.	42–48	3 shelves
2.	60–66	4–5 shelves
3.	72–82	6 shelves
4.	84–90	7 shelves

Note: Shelving heights vary slightly from manufacturer to manufacturer.

C. Shelving depths (in inches)

1.	10	Standard
2.	12	Reference and picture books
3.	15	Multimedia

D. Shelving capacity estimates (approximately ¾ full)

1.	Nonfiction	8 books per linear foot
2.	Fiction	10 books per linear foot
3.	Reference	6 books per linear foot
4.	Juvenile fiction and nonfiction	13 books per linear foot
5.	Picture books	20 books per linear foot
6.	Children's reference books	8 books per linear foot

E

Recommended Chair and Table Heights

A. Chair seat heights (in inches)

1.	K–Grade 2	12–14
2.	Grades 3–4	15–16
3.	Grades 5–6	16–18
4.	Grades 7 and up	17–18
5.	Height-adjustable task chairs	
	K–Grade 4	14–17
	Grade 5 and up	16–20.5

B. Table heights (in inches)

1.	K–Grade 2	22–23
2.	Grades 3–4	24–26
3.	Grades 5–6	26–29
4.	Grades 7–12	29
5.	Computer workstation	26–29
	Ideal keyboard height	26.5
6.	Computer, stand-up height	39
7.	Wheelchair accessible, adult	28–34
	K–Grade 5	26–29

C. Seat height to table height distance (in inches)

1.	Preschool, kindergarten, and grade 1	8–10
2.	Grades 2–12	10–11

These distances may need to be adjusted to allow sufficient leg clearance at tables with aprons.

APPENDIX

F

Sample Furniture Specification

Item:	Library Table
Quantity:	16
Furniture plan location:	#5
Dimensions:	42" wide × 42" long × 29" high

Description: *Tabletop:* 1¼" thick 3-ply 45-lb. density particleboard core. Particleboard must be formed of wood chips bonded with a water-resistant adhesive. It must have a minimum average modulus of rupture of 2,400 PSI and a minimum average modulus of elasticity of 400,000 PSI. 0.0509 high-pressure laminate face with a phenolic impregnated backing sheet not less than 0.0289. Laminate treated to provide superior abrasion and scuff resistance. Core externally banded on all four sides with solid oak ⅝" thick × 1⁹⁄₁₆" radiused ⅞" to form a bullnose edge splined and glued to the core material. Bands set flush to laminate. Four corners sectored to provide a uniform ⅝" thick band detail. No reveals or vein lines are permitted at the joint.

Legs: Legs constructed of one solid piece of select northern-grown red oak 2⅜" square with a ¾" radius applied on all four edges. Bottom of legs bored for a propeller nut internally threaded to receive an adjustable glide.

Leg Assembly: Metal-to-metal leg-to-top joint that consists of a metal plate with a ⁵⁄₁₆" minimum thickness. Plate is attached to the tabletop with a minimum of four machine bolts that pass through the plate and thread into metal bushings embedded in the tabletop. Plate is anchored to the leg with a minimum of two machine bolts that pass through the steel plate and thread into a ⅝" steel dowel nut that is embedded crosswise into the upper portion of the leg. Plates painted flat black with no sharp edges.

Glides: Each leg fitted with a rustproof nickel-plated adjustable glide no less than 1³⁄₁₆" in diameter × ½" thick.

Miscellaneous: Table must be of true apronless design with a 27³⁄₁₆" minimum vertical clearance to the underside of the top.

All exposed wood parts must be of northern-grown red oak free of imperfections and carefully selected for uniformity of grain. Wood must be air dried for a period of not less than six months and subsequently kiln dried to a final moisture content of 6% to 8%. The kiln drying process must employ National Hardwood Assn. standards.

Colors and Finishes: *Wood Finish:* Black on oak

Prior to finishing, all components must be thoroughly inspected for imperfections. Any small imperfections found will be carefully filled, hand sanded, and then cleaned. Finally, a finish system will be applied consisting of stain, followed by two applications of an ultraviolet cured coating, electrostatically applied.

Laminate: Wilsonart 467360 Saffron Tigris

APPENDIX

G

Sources of Furniture and Fixtures

Library Furniture/Shelving Manufacturers

Agati
312-829-1977
http://www.agati.com

Blanton and Moore
704-528-4506
http://www.blantonandmoore.com

Bretford Manufacturing, Inc.
888-521-1884
http://www.bretford.com

Brodart Company
800-820-4377
http://www.brodart.com

The Buckstaff Company
800-755-5890
http://www.buckstaff.com

Demco
800-962-4463
http://www.demco.com

ENEM Systems by Harrier
Interior Products Corp.
847-934-1310
http://www.harrierproducts.com

Fetzers
801-484-6103
http://www.fetzersinc.com

Gaylord Bros.
800-448-6160
http://www.gaylord.com

Highsmith
800-558-2110
http://www.highsmith.com

Library Bureau
800-221-6638
http://www.librarybureau.com

Mohawk Library Furniture
847-570-0448
http://www.mohawkfurniture.us/
portal/tabID_3326/DesktopDefault.aspx

Texwood Furniture Company
888-878-0000
http://www.texwood.com

Thos. Moser Cabinetmakers
800-708-9045
http://www.thosmoser.com
    specializes in solid-wood construction

TMC Furniture
734-622-0080
http://www.tmcfurniture.com

TotaLibra
800-243-0464
http://www.totalibra.com
    *European-inspired furniture
    and shelving systems*

The Worden Company
800-748-0561
http://www.wordencompany.com

Additional Shelving Manufacturers

Estey/Tennsco
800-251-8184
http://www.tennsco.com

Library Bureau Steel
856-696-5700
http://www.librarybureausteel.com

MJ Industries
800-247-4353
http://www.mjshelving.com

Montel
877-935-0236
http://www.montel.com

Spacesaver Corp.
800-492-3434
http://www.spacesaver.com

Contract Furniture Manufacturers

Allsteel
888-255-7833
http://www.allsteeloffice.com

Blockhouse
800-346-1126
http://www.blockhouse.com
lounge seating

The Danko Design Initiative
866-950-5005
http://www.peterdanko.com

ERG International
800-446-1186
http://www.erginternational.com/
default.asp

Eustis Chair
978-827-3103
http://www.eustischair.com

Fixtures Furniture
800-821-3500
http://www.fixturesfurniture.com/
index.html

Group Four Furniture
877-585-1478
http://www.groupfourfurniture
.com

The Gunlocke Company
800-828-6300
http://www.gunlocke.com

Haworth
616-393-3000
http://www.haworth.com

Herman Miller
616-654-3000
http://www.hermanmiller.com

The HON Company
800-336-9212
http://www.honcompany.com

Howe
800-466-4808
http://www.howefurniture.com

Humanscale
800-400-0625
http://www.humanscale.com
ergonomic seating and products

ICF
800-237-1625
http://www.icfsource.com

Interior Concepts
800-678-5550
http://www.interiorconcepts.com
office partitions and office furniture

Jasper Chair Company
812-482-5239
http://www.jasperchair.com

KI Krueger International
800-424-2432
http://www.ki-inc.com

The Knoll Group
877-615-6655
http://www.knoll.com/knoll_home
.jsp

Leland International
800-859-7510
http://www.lelandinternational
.com

Loewenstein Furniture
954-960-1100
http://www.loewensteininc.com/
default.aspx
   lounge seating

Metro
510-567-5200
http://www.metrofurniture.com

Neutral Posture
800-446-3746
http://www.neutralposture.com

Sauder Manufacturing
800-537-1530
http://www.saudercontract.com

Sit On It
888-274-8664
http://www.sitonit.net
ergonomic seating

Steelcase
800-333-9939
http://www.steelcase.com

Thonet
800-873-3252
http://www.thonet.com

Virco
800-448-4726
http://www.virco.com

VS America
704-378-6500
http://www.vs-furniture.com

*Additional sources for contract
furniture can be found at http://www
.contractdesignsourceguide.com.*

Acoustical Products

Working Walls
216-749-7850
http://www.workingwalls.com

Children's Furniture Manufacturers

Big Cozy Books
925-447-1582
http://www.bigcozybooks.com
   *upholstered books for reading
   nook seating*

Donie Chair Company
800-732-8727
http://www.doniechair.com
   rocking chairs

Educational Furniture, Inc.
800-545-4474
http://www.kinderlink.com

Gressco, Ltd.
800-345-3480
http://www.gresscoltd.com

M2L
800-319-8222
http://www.m2lcollection.com
stackable cushions with removable/ washable fabric covers

Display Fixtures

Franklin Fixtures, Inc.
508-291-1475
http://www.franklinfixtures.com
bookstore furniture suitable for library display

Signage

APCO
877-988-2726
http://www.apcosigns.com

ASI Sign Systems, Inc.
800-274-7732
http://www.asisign.com

Theft-Detection Systems

Checkpoint Systems, Inc.
800-257-5540
http://www.checkpointlibrary.com

3M
888-364-3577
http://solutions.3m.com/wps/
portal/3M/en_US/library/home/
products/detection_systems/

Window Shading Systems

MechoShade Systems
718-729-2020
http://www.mechoshade.com

Hunter Douglas
800-727-8953
http://www.hunterdouglascontract
.com/home.jsp

Miscellaneous

Doug Mockett & Company
800-523-1269
http://www.mockett.com/default
.asp?ID=2&Check=True
architectural hardware and wire management

Kelly Computer Supply Company
651-773-1109
http://www.kellyrest.com
ergonomic and desktop accessories

Peter Pepper Products
800-496-0204
http://www.peterpepperproducts
.com
clocks, coat trees, magazine racks, planters, display cases, trash receptacles

Smith System
972-398-4050
http://www.smithsystem.com
book trucks, book carts, computer furniture

APPENDIX

H

Useful Websites

http://www.asumag.com
American School and University Magazine: Information on school facilities planning and an annual "Educational Interiors Showcase" facilities design competition

http://www.access-board.gov/adaag/html/adaag.htm
ADA Accessibility Guidelines for Buildings and Facilities (ADAAG)

http://www.usdoj.gov/crt/ada/adahom1.htm
Americans with Disabilities Act (ADA) Home Page

http://www.chps.net
The Collaborative for High Performance Schools

http://www.orosha.org/cergos/index.html
Computer Ergonomics for Elementary School

http://ergo.human.cornell.edu
Cornell University Ergonomics Web: Ergonomics information and research studies. Of particular interest is "School Ergonomics Programs: Guidelines for Parents."

http://www.designshare.com
DesignShare: The International Forum for Innovative Schools

http://www.education.umn.edu/kls/ecee/default.html
Ergonomics for Children and Educational Environments (International Ergonomics Association): A forum for the exchange of information related to children and educational environments

http://data.webjunction.org/ct/documents/6181.pdf
Library Space Planning Guide, Connecticut State Library

http://www.librisdesign.org/docs/index.html
Libris Design Planning Documentation: Documents on library facilities planning

http://www.edfacilities.org/rl/libraries.cfm
National Clearinghouse for Educational Facilities (NCEF): Library and Media Center Facilities Design—K–12

http://www.slais.ubc.ca/resources/architecture/index.htm
Planning and Building Libraries: Online resources on all aspects of planning and building libraries from the University of British Columbia

http://www.resources.com
ReSources.Com: Information on the contract furniture industry, including a directory of manufacturers

http://www.peterli.com/spm/
School Planning and Management: Information on school facilities planning and archives from *School Planning and Management* magazine

http://www.webjunction.org/do/DisplayContent?id=12748
WebJunction's Focus on Space Planning for Libraries

http://www.wbdg.org/design/school_library.php
Whole Building Design Guide: School Library

http://www.workspace-resources.com
WorkSpace Resources: Information on contract furniture, ergonomics, and design. An education section provides information on technology and classroom/instruction room design.

http://www.ala.org/ala/yalsa/profdev/spaces.htm
YA Spaces: Resources on young adult spaces in libraries from the Young Adult Library Services Association

Selected Readings

Planning and Renovating School Library Facilities

Brown, Carol R. *Interior Design for Libraries: Drawing on Function and Appeal.* Chicago: American Library Association, 2002.

Doll, Carol A. "School Library Media Centers: The Human Environment." *School Library Media Quarterly* (Summer 1992): 225–29.

Focke, John. "Beyond Books: The Expanding Role of Media Centers." *The High School Magazine* (May/June 1998): 36–41.

Johnson, Doug. "Building Digital Libraries for Analog People: 10 Common Design Pitfalls and How to Avoid Them." *Knowledge Quest* (March/April 2000). http://www.doug-johnson.com/dougwri/diglib.html.

Maine Association of School Libraries Facilities Committee. *Maine School Libraries Facilities Handbook.* Maine Association of School Libraries, 1999. http://www.maslibraries.org/about/facilities/handbook.html.

Meyerberg, Henry. "School Libraries: A Design Recipe for the Future." *KQ on the Web* 31, no. 1 (September/October 2002). http://www.ala.org/ala/aasl/aaslpubsandjournals/kqweb/kqarchives/volume31/311myerberg.htm.

Meyers, E. "The Coolness Factor: Ten Libraries Listen to Youth." *American Libraries* (November 1999): 10.

O'Neill, Lucinda M. "Building Forward: How Communities Can Design School or Public Libraries That Will Serve This Generation and the Next." *Threshold* (Winter 2004). http://www.ciconline.org/c/document_library/get_file?folderId=35&name=W04-buildingforward.pdf.

Schneider, Mark. *Do School Facilities Affect Academic Outcomes?* Washington, DC: National Clearinghouse for Educational Facilities, November 2002. http://www.edfacilities.org/pubs/outcomes.pdf.

Taney, Kimberly Bolan. *Teen Spaces: The Step-by-Step Library Makeover.* Chicago: American Library Association, 2003.

Trelease, J. "What's New: Reflections on the 'New' Book Stores." *Trelease-on-Reading.com* (March 10, 2001). http://www.trelease-on-reading.com/whatsnu_4.html.

Truett, Carol. "A Survey of School and Public Children's Library Facilities: What Librarians Like, Dislike, and Most Want to Change about Their Libraries." *School Library Media Quarterly* (Winter 1994): 91–97.

Woodward, Jeannette. *Creating the Customer-Driven Library: Building on the Bookstore Model.* Chicago: American Library Association, 2005.

Working with Architects

Bradley, William S. "Working with an Architect to Design Your School." *School Executive* (November/December 1998): 10.

Fenton, Serena. "Architectural Follies." *School Library Journal* (February 1999): 26–29.

Rockwell, Eric. "The Seven Deadly Sins of Architects: Gluttony and Lust Aren't on the List—But Ignorance and Myopia in Library Design Are." *American Libraries* (April 1989): 307–9.

Program Planning

American Association of School Librarians and Association for Educational Communications and Technology. *Information Power: Building Partnerships for Learning.* Chicago: American Library Association, 1998.

Bolch, Matt. "Not Your Father's Library." *Scholastic Administrator* (May 2006). http://www.scholastic .com/administrator/may06/articles.asp?article= Library.

Brown, Robert A. "Students as Partners in Library Design." *School Library Journal* (February 1992): 31–34.

Hughes-Hassell, Sandra, and Anne Wheelock, eds. *The Information-Powered School.* Chicago: American Library Association (Public Education Network and American Association of School Librarians), 2001.

Loertscher, David. "The Digital School Library: A World-wide Development and a Fascinating Challenge." *Teacher Librarian* (June 2003). http:// www.teacherlibrarian.com/tlmag/v_30/v_30_5_ feature.html.

Loertscher, David V. *Reinvent Your School's Library in the Age of Technology: A Guide for Principals and Superintendents.* San Jose, CA: Hi Willow Research and Publishing, 1998.

McKenzie, Jamie. "The Techno-Savvy, Book-Rich Media Center." *Library Media Connection* (November/December 2003). http://www.fno.org/ apr04/technosavvy.html.

Oatman, Eric. "Overwhelming Evidence: Now, There's a Surefire Way to Show How Libraries Make a Big Difference in Students' Lives." *School Library Journal* (January 2006): 56–59.

Oblinger, Diana G., and James L. Oblinger, eds. *Educating the Net Generation.* An Educause eBook, 2005. http://www.educause.edu/books/ educatingthenetgen/5989.

Planning for School Library Resource Centers (ERS Info-File WS-5327). Alexandria, VA: Educational Research Service.

Results That Matter: 21st Century Skills and High School Reform. Tucson, AZ: Partnership for 21st Century Skills, March 2006. http://www.21stcenturyskills .org/documents/RTM2006.pdf.

Woolls, Blanche, and David Loertscher, eds. *The Whole School Library Handbook.* Chicago: American Library Association, 2004.

Technology Planning: Theft-Detection Systems

"Resolution on Radio Frequency Identification (RFID) Technology and Privacy Principles." ALA Council, January 19, 2005. http://www.ala.org/ala/oif/ statementspols/ifresolutions/rfidresolution.htm.

Space Planning

Building Blocks for Library Space: Functional Guidelines. Chicago: Library Administration and Management Association, American Library Association, 1995.

Johnson, Doug. "A Jolt of Java @ Your Library." *Blue Skunk Blog* (October 13, 2005). http:// doug-johnson.squarespace.com/blue-skunk-blog/2005/10/13/a-jolt-of-java-your-library.html.

Valenza, Joyce Kasman. "Library as Multimedia Studio: Top Ten Reasons to Move Production out of the Lab and into the Stacks." *Electronic Learning* (November/December 1996): 56–57.

Elementary School Libraries (Robin Hood Foundation Library Initiative)

Kolleeny, Jane. "The Library Goes Back to School." *Architectural Record* (September 2005). http://archrecord.construction.com/people/profiles/archives/0509RobinHoodFoundation-1.asp.

Pedersen, Martin C., and Paul Makovsky. "Power of Place: A School Play." *Metropolis Magazine* (October 2002). http://www.metropolismag.com/html/content_1002/lib/index.html.

Schibsted, Evantheia. "Way Beyond Fuddy-Duddy." *Edutopia* (October 2005). http://www.edutopia.org/magazine/ed1article.php?id=art_1354&issue=oct_05#.

Weeks, Katie. "Reading Room." *Contract* (June 2006): 104–7.

Furniture

Brown, Carol R. *Planning Library Interiors: The Selection of Furnishings for the 21st Century.* Phoenix: Oryx Press, 1995.

Lighting

Grocoff, Paul N. "Electric Lighting and Daylighting in Schools." *CEFPI IssueTrak* (December 1995). http://www.cefpi.org/issue1.html.

Ries, Jack. "Nine Steps to a Successful Lighting Retrofit." *School Planning and Management* (December 1998): 29. http://www.peterli.com/archive/spm/816.shtm.

Schlipf, Fred, and John Moorman. "Let There Be at Least Half-Way Decent Light: How Library Illumination Systems Work—and Don't Work." Summary of a presentation at the Public Library Association Conference in Phoenix, 2002. http://www.urbanafreelibrary.org/departments/presentations/lighting/fredlights.pdf

Zuczek, Daniel. "Illuminating Classroom Design." *American School and University* (July 1996): 40–42.

Ergonomics

Butler, Sharon. "Common-Sense Ergonomics (or, What You Don't Do Can Hurt You!)." *Computers in Libraries* (September 1997): 35–37.

Rasicot, Julie. "Ergonomics 101: How to Guard against Health Problems in the Computer Lab." *Electronic School* (January 2000). http://www.electronic-school.com/2000/01/0100f2.html.

Accessibility

Walling, Linda Lucas. "Granting Each Equal Access." *School Library Media Quarterly* (Summer 1992): 216–22.

Wojahn, Rebecca Hogue. "Everyone's Invited." *School Library Journal* (February 2006): 46–48.

Signage

Yeaman, Andrew. "Lost in the Information Supermarket." *Wilson Library Journal* (December 1999): 42–46, 89.

Learning Styles

Kussrow, Paul K., and Lucy Harrison. "Learning Styles in the Library: All Students Are Equal but Some Are More Equal Than Others." *Florida Libraries* (November/December 1997).

Specifications and Bid Documents

Baule, Steven M. "Developing Bid Specifications for Facilities Projects." *Knowledge Quest* 31, no. 1 (September/October 2002). http://www.ala.org/ala/aasl/aaslpubsandjournals/kqweb/kqarchives/volume31/311baule.htm.

Moving

Lehman, Kathy. "Promoting Library Advocacy and Information Literacy from an 'Invisible Library.'" *Teacher Librarian* (April 2002). http://www.teacherlibrarian.com/tlmag/v_29/v_29_4_feature.html.

Smallwood, Carol. "A Moving Checklist for Do-It-Yourselfers." *Book Report* (January/February 1998): 12–13.

Joint School-Public Libraries

Bundy, A. "For the Public Good: Joint Use Libraries in Australia and New Zealand." Adelaide: University of South Australia Library, December 1999. http://www.library.unisa.edu.au/about/papers/public.pdf.

———. "Joint-Use Libraries: The Ultimate Form of Cooperation." In *Planning the Modern Public Library Building*, ed. Gerard B. McCabe and James R. Kennedy. Westport, CT: Libraries Unlimited, 2003. Available at http://www.library.unisa.edu.au/about/papers/jointuse.pdf.

Combined School and Public Library Decision Making, 2nd ed. Madison: Wisconsin Department of Public Instruction, Division for Libraries and Community Learning, 1998. http://dpi.wi.gov/pld/pdf/comblibs.pdf.

Keller, S., and J. Waters, eds. *Joint Ventures: The Promise, Power and Performance of Partnering*. Sacramento: California State Library, 2001. http://www.library.ca.gov/assets/acrobat/JointVentures.pdf.

Kratz, C. "Joint-Use Libraries: Thinking Out of the Box." *College and Research Libraries News* (March 2000): 61–62.

Index

Rolf Erikson has been a school library facility consultant for fifteen years and has consulted on over eighty projects for public and independent schools, both in the United States and internationally. He has thirty years' experience as a school library media specialist at all levels, K–12. Most recently, he was school library director at Minuteman Regional High School in Lexington, Massachusetts. Previously, he was director of library and audiovisual services at the Frankfurt International School in Oberursel, Germany. His professional experience also includes K–12 classroom teaching. He has an M.S. in instructional technology from the University of Wisconsin–Stout and a B.A. in art education from Concordia College, Moorhead, Minnesota. He has presented workshops on school library design for national, regional, and state professional library organizations, and has taught courses on school library facilities design at the graduate level.

Carolyn Markuson is founder and president of biblioTECH, which offers consulting services to schools, public libraries, and regional library systems. Previously she was supervisor of libraries for the Brookline, Massachusetts, school district. Her professional experience includes working in several school, public, and special library environments as well as holding leadership positions in state, regional, and national professional library organizations. She has a doctorate in curriculum media and technology from Boston University and a C.A.G.S. (Public Administration) and an M.L.S. from Rutgers University. As a librarian, system director, and consultant, she has worked with school systems, librarians, and architects both in the United States and abroad to design school library facilities that facilitate learning and welcome students. Most recently, she has been involved in the development of community library projects in the northeast in which both school and public libraries function in a single facility. In addition to facilities design, her consulting services have included the development of strategic plans, and comprehensive school library program evaluations for school systems seeking state-of-the-art school libraries.